MW01181831

VISION QUEST

Michael J Wager

VISION QUEST

DR. MICHAEL T. MAYO

Queens Army LLC   Tucson, Arizona

Copyright © 2020 by Michael T. Mayo

All rights are reserved. No part of this book may be copied, shared, stored, reproduced, or transmitted electronically or by any other means without explicit written permission from its creator Dr. Mayo

ISBN 978-1-7345741-0-4

Library of Congress Control Number: 2020901880

Published by: Queens Army LLC

2300 N. Craycroft Rd. #5

Tucson, Arizona 85712

Our website is: queensarmy.net

Pictures on front and back covers are courtesy of PIXABAY

Distributed by Ingram

Date of first printing, February 2020

Contents

Introduction

Many cultures incorporate the quest for visions as part of their rite of passage from childhood into full adult status. Visions are believed to have profound spiritual, religious and prophetic significance. This was my quest. These are my visions. This is my story.

Native American Proverb

Listen to the wind.
It talks.

Listen to the silence.
It speaks.

Listen to your heart.
It knows.

Dr. Mayo's Mantra

Nothing is what it appears to be, ever.

Don't take it personally, even if it's meant to be.

Every challenge brings an opportunity. (a gift).

The secret is to focus on the opportunity...
    Not on the challenge.

Expect nothing,
    and you will never be disappointed.

The only thing between you, and your dreams,
    is you.

Give yourself permission to fail... So you can
    give yourself permission to succeed.

Treat yourself the way you want others
    to treat you.

Learn to say 'Thank You,' and mean it.

Forgive others...
    So you can forgive yourself.

Baboquivari Peak

Baboquivari Peak is located in a 2,065 acre wilderness area in Southern Arizona. It is the sacred mountain for Tohono O'odham Indians. The word Baboquivari is an Anglicized version of the Tohono O'odam name meaning, a neck between two heads. This morning I decided to re-visit an event that I experienced there at the base of this sacred mountain many years ago.

On that morning when I awoke I found myself at the base of Baboquivari Peak. There was a clump of very tall prairie grass next to me. We do not have prairie grass in the desert of Southern Arizona. For some reason unknown to me, I began to dance around stomping my feet on this clump of prairie grass. When I stopped and looked up there was a young man, a teenager, staring at me. I recognized him. He was the youngest son of an assistant who worked with me at the time. His name is Matthew. This is the story his mother told me when I asked her about encountering her son at the base of the sacred mountain.

She said that Matthew was hunting there at the base of Baboquivari Peak that morning when he came face to face with a white buffalo with the face of a human, but there are no buffalo in Southern Arizona.

This morning I woke up at 3:45 a.m. I decided to go on an adventure on the night train that comes by at 4:00 o'clock. Because I had a few extra minutes before the train was to arrive, I sat down on the driveway instead of standing and waiting for the train to come by. Viewing the process unfolding from this vantage point seemed to provide me with greater clarity and detail. I was so focused on the process of the street and houses disappearing and the rail bed, crossties and tracks forming that I didn't notice the train coming until it was already slowing to a stop right in front of me. This train was different. It was not the passenger train which normally comes. It was a freight train pulling a long string of cattle-cars. When the conductor got down from the first car he was wearing a striped blue and white hat just like the engineer. His shirt was light blue and he was wearing striped blue and white overalls. In his left hand he held a railroad lantern. When I told the conductor where I wanted to go, he told me to tell the engineer what I wanted. The Engineer told me to stand on the cattle pusher at the front of the steam engine and hold on.

We moved slowly down the tracks for a while. The train stopped where a white buffalo was standing between the tracks facing us. I got off the train. The train disappeared. The white buffalo was still standing facing me in the middle of where the tracks had been moments before. The white buffalo bowed its head to me and I bowed my head to it. When I looked up there was a shirtless Indian standing facing me where the white buffalo had just been. He was completely covered in white dust. He was wearing buckskin pants and moccasins. He had a headband around his head with two feathers sticking up in the back. The feathers were not from an eagle or a hawk or an owl. They were from some different kind of bird that I wasn't familiar with. He was a few inches taller than me. He took my hand and led me to a small fire pit where several rocks formed a circle around a small pile of glowing coals. He sat down close to the fire facing east, northeast. I sat down facing him in just the opposite direction, west, southwest. He picked up a bunch of dried prairie grass and placed it onto the burning coals. Thick smoke billowed up and turned into a Grizzly Bear. The bear turned his lips up like only a grizzly can do and opened his mouth very wide and swallowed me.

When I opened my eyes I was in tall prairie grass somewhere in the Midwest. A young Indian boy about six years old wearing buckskin pants with no shoes on was standing next to me holding my hand. I too was wearing buckskin pants and had no shoes on. I was pink-white and he was red-brown. He led me to a small stream. We stepped over the small stream. On the other side everything was burned black, still smoldering from the ravages of a prairie fire. The ground was extremely hot and I began dancing around in an attempt to cool my burning feet. The Indian boy too began to dance and as he did so we both turned into prairie hens. I recognized the tail feathers of the prairie chicken. They were the same as the two feathers in the headband of the Indian man I had just encountered on my return visit to the sacred mountain, Baboquivari. He was obviously a shape shifter like me and he had shared his story through the magic smoke from burning prairie grass.

Matthew Gallaher is now a young man in his thirties. He still lives in Tucson, Arizona. He might be willing to tell you the story of his encounter with the white buffalo with the face of a man, if you offer him a cold beer and a kind ear.

Making Smoke

This morning, while I was contemplating whether I should get up yet, or continue to drag my feet about it, this apparition appeared above me. I recognized this character from a past encounter, many years ago. "Aren't you that smoke guy," I asked? He said that he was the Smoke Chief. He was Native American, dressed from head to toe in buckskin, wearing a full feather headdress. I asked why he was there. He said that he had come to show me how to 'make smoke.'

He took a pinch of dried, shredded tobacco, dipped his fingers in water and formed the tobacco into little cones. After making several of these small cones, he went back to the first one and began modifying the cones by forcing his thumb into their base, leaving a small indentation. "Let these cones dry before you light them," he said. Next he took a flattened piece of what he said was the inside core from a cactus plant. It was about the size and shape of a stick of butter, sliced in half longwise and then lain side by side. He began wrapping a strip of cactus fiber around and around the cactus-core. He started winding in the center and moved toward its base, then back to the center and up towards its top. The end result resembled a small bowling pin about six inches tall with its bottom quarter cut off.

He said to use these as a base upon which to place the tobacco cones, before you lite them with the burning end of a dried reed. He illustrated this process by setting up several of these units around a sick person, who was lying on a pallet on the ground. He said that the smoke could be used to see what was wrong with a sick person, or to see into the future. I asked if it was all right to use store bought tobacco. He said, "No way. You have to use wild tobacco, or grow your own from seed, then air dry them and shred them, or shred them while they're still green, and then dry the leaves."

He said that he would return to show me how to use smoke to 'see into the future.' Then he vanished.

I thought about this for a while. I came to the conclusion that the Smoke Chief had come because I had been working on getting the basics down on how to use 'The Event Horizon' to see future events before they happen for almost a week now, but with only modest success.

Red Face, Red Man

This morning, late, about 4:30 a.m., I saw an eye, from a side angle perspective. Eyes are almost always portals to something, or somewhere. I never pass up an opportunity to see what lies behind an eye, no matter how tired I am.

I entered the eye, and there in front of me was a red face. Not devil red and not barn red, but a really tanned red, like only a real purebred Plains Indian could possibly have. His skin appeared to be really weathered. His face had sunken cheeks, free of any surplus fat. His salt and pepper gray hair was bound around with a leather strap. A couple of feathers and various other curiosities adorned his thick locks that trailed down behind his back. His deerskin attire was as weathered as the thin skin on the back of his hands. They moved deftly. His right hand held a hand carved wooden spoon, while the left hand held an elongated dried gourd bowl. He put a spoonful of refried pinto beans into the bowl, then a couple of spoons full of boiled white rice, followed by two slices of yellow squash, and finally the end of a green onion with all of its roots intact, which had been boiled until it was completely cooked.

After the bowl was filled, the Red Man turned and kneeled down next to the same infirmed man that was on the pallet, on the floor, in 'Making Smoke.' He then stuffed all of the food into the sick man's mouth and forced him to eat it all. Then he started hitting the sick man on his chest with the same wooden spoon, which he just finished using to stuff the food into the man's mouth.

A hole opened up in the man's chest and out flew what looked like a black bat with a long lizard-like tail. Closely behind this bat-like creature came pairs of brown clumps of something. Pair after pair of these clumps trailed away after the bat-like creature, as it disappeared into the sky. After nine or ten of these pairs had left the man's chest and vanished, the opening in the man's chest closed leaving no sign that it had been there. The comatose man opened his eyes and looked around.

The entire scene vanished in the blink of an eye. I was again in my own bed staring up at a dark blank ceiling.

Normal Day

I took my Cardigan Welsh Corgi for his morning walk at a quarter to seven. We went down an alley where there was a large antique Indian burial pot, discarded. I inspected the pot and determined that it was cracked badly in several places. It was hand made and rather irregular and crudely made at that, unglazed and black from being fired in an open charcoal pit. As

I left, it was obvious to me that something had come out of the pot and was riding on my back. It turned out to be 'The Spirit of the Pot.' It accompanied me until we got to my house. I told 'The Spirit of the Pot' that it was welcome to stay in my front yard, as long as it didn't cause any problems. The spirit told me that it could no longer stay in that pot because the pot was broken and it was being discarded.

It turns out that this spirit can manipulate the sense of time. That is, it can give one the sense that an event of short duration can seem very long or a long event can seem very short. Perhaps a spirit like this may turn out to be helpful in the future. One never knows.

September 11th turned out to be a normal day after all. There were no beheadings of American journalists today.

The Spirit in the Pot

The Spirit in the Pot told me it needed to be in a dark, protected space in some kind of container, for it to feel safe. So, I put it in one of the large ceramic Fu dogs which we have protecting the entrance to our house. My wife was not happy about having any more spirits around our house, even if the spirits were kept in the front yard. She wanted me to get rid of the spirit and for sure, to leave that ancient burial pot alone where it was abandoned in the alley.

I went out to catch the Night Bus that would be coming by at 2:00 o'clock in the morning and asked the Spirit if it would like to go along with me. It said, "Definitely not!" So, I went out to the curb and waited for the bus to come. When the bus stopped and the driver opened the door, I asked the driver if he could take the Spirit in the Pot somewhere safe and help me to get rid of it. He looked puzzled, scratched his head with his raccoon fingers, gave it some thought and shook his head affirmatively up and down slowly.

I ran back to the Fu dog and grabbed the spirit. We jumped onto the bus and the driver started moving slowly down the street. He took a ninety-degree turn to the left which he had never done before. Then we entered a large tunnel. There were florescent lights strung intermittently along the ceiling in three rows. We kept gaining speed until the lights appeared to be a continuous blur, then the whole ceiling appeared to be completely illuminated. When we finally stopped and departed the bus, everything was just light, as though there were fog being illuminated from every direction, as though the fog itself was emitting light.

As we departed the bus the Spirit was transformed into a beautiful Indian maiden. She was dressed entirely in deerskin. Her dark hair was tightly braided in two long braids. The ends were wound tightly with strings of tiny beads of many colors for about one and one half inches near the very ends of the braids. Each braid was also secured at its base above her ears where the braids began by a wrapping of colored fibers. These appeared to be made of wool or bison hair spun or twisted into yarn. Her moccasins were very high and covered her lower legs completely. They had one large silver button on the outside of each moccasin. The upper portions of her moccasins were laced together with leather strips. Her skirt was long, well below the knee. Her long sleeve jacket came below her waist. It had decorative fringe several inches long down the back of each arm. There were several ceremonial silver bangles hanging from long leather strips adorning her jacket. She must have been the daughter of some high-ranking member of her tribe. My guess would be that she probably came from one of the plains tribes, possibly from Oklahoma. She was a very pretty young lady.

The Indian princess said that a powerful medicine man had imprisoned her spirit in the large pot and buried it in a cave. She didn't know what happened to her body and she had no idea how long she had been in the burial pot. My guess and that is only a guess, would be that she had been there for a couple of hundred years. She had no knowledge of the white man. She was so thankful to me for liberating her and bringing her here to the 'confluence of lights.' She came over to where I was sitting and kissed me on the forehead. Then into the fog of light disappeared the beautiful Indian Princess.

Indian in a Pot

City refuse collection is twice each year in our neighborhood. They pick up any unwanted items left in the alley. It seemed inappropriate for me to allow that large discarded, historic Indian Pot to be squashed and taken away to the City Dump, just because it was cracked. The fact that the pot contained the spirit of an Indian Princess for so many years just added to my dilemma. My wife didn't want me to bring the pot home. I didn't think it should be left in the alley, so I took it to the office for safe keeping, until I could find a home for it. One of the girls at the office placed a purple rosary in the pot, with most of the beads hanging out over its edge. Another of the girls at the office said that she had heard loud noises when she was there alone. It sounded like someone had entered the premises and was rummaging around in back but no one was there when she went to investigate.

I needed to get to the bottom of this situation with the 'Indian in the Pot.' I went in search of the Indian Princess who had come from the pot in question and disappeared into the fog of light. I eventually found her hiding in a deciduous forest. She was all dirty. Her deerskin clothing was badly torn and she had lost both of her moccasins.

I took her down to the river to bathe, while I got rid of the ragged clothing she had been wearing. She seemed to trust me completely, perhaps because I had already rescued her once from the pot in which she was imprisoned. When she came out of the river, I clothed her in a floor-length white silk dress, with a long, white silk scarf covering her dark waist-length braided hair.

Out of the forest, burst a very muscular Indian Warrior who was wearing buckskin trousers. His chest was bare. His head was partially shaven, with a long dark braid of hair protruding from the right side of his head above and behind his ear. He had a gold or copper band around his left bicep and a leather band tied with a thong around his right bicep. On his forehead he wore what looked like a red sweat band made of some kind of material tied in back of his head in a double knot. His face was twisted and angry. He cried out in a loud voice, "She is mine." He drew a large knife from beneath the leather belt around his waist as he moved towards me. He was way bigger than I am.

I summoned Raymond, the magic horse. He instantly materialized out of thin air. The Indian stopped in his tracks, frozen as though he had never even seen a horse before. This magnificent specimen is truly a huge horse, standing twenty hands at the shoulder and very muscular. I swept the Indian Princess up and onto the bare back of the horse, placing her sidesaddle, clinging to its long mane. The Indian cried out again, "She belongs to me, Many Wolves."

Never tell a sorcerer your name. I summoned a pack of six wolves that immediately began circling around the Indian Warrior with their teeth bared, growling in unison, staring him down. Raymond, the magic horse, the Indian Princess and I transported to where her family lived, leaving the angry Indian Warrior encircled by six hungry wolves. Her father approached with great excitement upon seeing his beautiful daughter. The only thing he said to me was, "Many Moons!" I don't know if his name was Many Moons or her name was Many Moons or if it had been many moons since he had last seen his daughter. I left them united in eternity and my office and the pot free of all spirits. It's all in a day's work for a sorcerer like me.

Long Bow

Last night, or more correctly, this morning at 1:00 o'clock, I went out to the street to catch a ride with Maurice, in his red & black biplane. I heard a plane coming in the distance but it didn't sound like the old biplane's engine. The sound tapered off quickly and was barely audible. Whatever kind of plane that was coming was lined up for a direct approach, with its engine throttled way down. It had landing lights, so I knew for sure, that it wasn't the old biplane. It touched down at the end of our street. The engines were shut down completely, as soon as the wheels touched the ground. I knew immediately that it was a C-47 or DC-3. It stopped directly in front of me. I went around to the other side of the plane and climbed up the ladder into the fuselage. It was a DC-3, but there were no seats in the bay area, so it must be used for hauling cargo. It was completely empty at the moment. I made my way up to the cockpit and sat down in the right seat. The captain was sitting in the left seat. He looked very familiar, even with his flight cap pulled down low on his forehead, his earphones covering his ears, and his aviator sunglasses covering his eyes, though it was quite dark outside. His thin dark mustache and chiseled features gave away his identity. This was Howard Hughes, in his prime. He turned and faced me but didn't say a word.

I told him I wanted to go someplace I needed to go to. I told him I needed to see something I needed to see. I told him I needed to know something I needed to know. He stared at me for a moment, then, he barked, "Grab the yoke. Push the throttle quadrant all the way forward. Move the yoke forward when the airspeed hits 40 knots. As soon as the tail comes up pull back on the yoke give it a little left rudder and keep the nose five degrees above the horizon. Straight out departure until airspeed reaches 170 knots. Make a shallow turn to port, until we reach 5 degrees magnetic heading. Climb to flight level 115. Pull back on the throttle quadrant and keep the RPM's at 1800. Watch the cylinder head temperatures. Don't run the engines too lean. Turn on the oxygen if you get light-headed. Maintain our airspeed between 175 and 180 knots, straight on till morning. I'll be asleep. Don't bother me unless there is an emergency."

As dawn broke to the east, I could see foothills and mountains in the distance. The captain began to stir as the darkness of night receded. He scanned the horizon, pointed at an expanse of grassland to the right of the foothills and said, "Good job. I'm going to put her down right there at the base of that mountain."

We were greeted by a friendly band of Indians. They had never seen an airplane before, so they treated us as royalty and invited us to join them in celebration and dance around their communal fire pit that evening. As the festivities waned, the chief introduced himself to us as Long Bow. He also introduced his wife and all of the elders. When he asked if we would smoke the ritual tribal peace pipe as a sign of friendship, I produced the peace pipe that was given to me by the father of the Indian Princess, I rescued from the pot. Long Bow exclaimed in great excitement, "This magnificent peace pipe you have could have only been made by someone from our tribe!" Then I filled the bowl of my peace pipe with the tribe's own tobacco and began to puff it, the smoke became a full size likeness of the beautiful Indian Princess. Long Bow sprang to his feet and cried out, "She is my Grandmother Many Moons!" Howard Hughes had brought us to the Black Hills of South Dakota. This was her tribe. This is where the pot belongs.

Cave-Rock

Last night I asked the Source if it was all right for us to visit concession number twenty-one. He said it should be O. K. for us to visit that concession. We went straight away to concession twenty-one. When we arrived, there were seven black-hawks flying single file in close formation right over us, heading somewhere. This concession was a rookery for black-hawks. There were twenty more hawks waiting in line to join the other seven. That made a total of twenty-seven black-hawks in a hurry to get some place. I shape shifted into a hawk myself, an especially large one and very black at that, then I followed them to their destination.

We were in Navajo country, dry, and desolate, with little vegetation. We swooped down towards a large flat rock and passed under the exposed edge on the east side of the rock, right into a cave. Immediately I knew exactly where we were. This was the 'Cave of the East.' These creatures were 'spirit hawks.' They were shape shifting Navajo Medicine Men. They paid little attention to me. I watched intently as they prepared themselves for the ritual of entry into the spirit-world of the Navajo, through the sacred 'Cave of the East' whose whereabouts is known only to Medicine Men of the Navajo Nation. I followed behind them as they entered in silence and secrecy, single file, into the 'Spirit World of the Navajo.' I was anxious to discover the magic that lay hidden within the confines of this cave.

To a spelunker this cave would be called an alcove not a cavern, for here there were no tunnels, except the tunneling within their minds. Each of the medicine men held a bundle of coiled luminescent threads in their left hand. With their right hands they strung the glowing threads creating a pathway and forming a tunnel like an orb-spider spins its web. Out of the emptiness and darkness a luminescent, glowing cave emerged. I followed, as what was familiar descended into the unknown, the spirit world of the Navajo. This luminescent tunnel opened into the eternity of the Navajo past, where their memories re-united with the remembered. The plants, the animals, the people, the places, they all became their reality. They all became rememberings.

Navajo medicine men use these rememberings to re-connect to the past and use the power within that past to alter the present, just as a wizard uses the power of their imaginings to alter the present by connecting it to the future. A magician likewise uses the magic residing within everything to accomplish almost anything, while the shaman will dive deeply beneath the surface of the earth to gather their knowledge, wisdom and energy from Earth Mother.

Therein lies the importance of our history. Therein lies the value of historians, the validity of oral tradition and tribal rituals.

The medicine man blows smoke or spittle onto the sick or dying person or animal attempting to re-connect their wellness of the past to the un-wellness of the present through their rememberings blown out with their breath.

Only by remembering what we actually were, can we know who we truly are.

Wararies

Wednesday night I went to visit Dream Walker. I had not seen him for quite awhile. So, I journeyed to the gateway to his world. I sat down to wait for him to come because he always came in short order but he never showed up. I became quite concerned for his safety, so I entered through the gateway marked by the two large poles and began looking for him. I was very familiar with his world. He gave me the gift of dream walking. He taught me how to dream walk, and he showed me all of the rituals that went with its practice. I investigated his wigwam, his fire pit, his sacred places, but he was nowhere to be found. I sensed that he was near his sacred mountain that was actually a very large hill. There on the backside was the entrance to a cave that had not been present before. It was very dark and spooky inside.

The entrance to this lair was narrow and just tall enough for me to enter without ducking my head. I pulled out the glowing disc that I carry with me on a leather string around my neck. The light emitted from this disc is similar to the light from a full moon. For some reason, the light was being absorbed before it reached the walls of the cave. For additional lighting, I drew the glowing sword, with its shimmering reflective surfaces. It too failed to illuminate the cave walls. But, sets of yellow eyes could be seen reflected from the polished surface of the sword. As I moved deeper into the cave, it widened into a large central arena, where a single wooden pole protruded straight up out of the ground. Tied to the pole with heavy rope slumped the Dream Walker.

I approached the Dream Walker with caution, leaned down and whispered into his ear, "I'm going to cut you loose. Follow me out of here." There was no response. Next, I administered a secret potion that reverses the effects of any toxin. Again, there was no reaction. That's when I knew I would have to carry him out on my shoulder. I deftly cut the heavy ropes with the magical half sword and hoisted Dream Walker onto my shoulder. With the glowing disc dangling from the leather string around my neck and with my shimmering sword held tightly in my right hand, I turned around to make my way back out of the cave. Then I saw them. There were several of them blocking my path. They looked like skinny, black, giant gingerbread men with glowing yellow eyes. They had no noses, and no buttons or any other decorations, just three lips and two round yellow eyes. With slashing sword and swaying disc, we made for the entrance to the cave.

By the time I saw the light of day, I was panting

heavily. They failed to follow as we made for Dream Walker's home. I put his limp body down on the thin sleeping mat on the floor in the center of his wigwam. I was at a complete loss. I had no idea what to do for Dream Walker, but I knew that he wouldn't make it unless something was done for him. I had to leave. I had to get help.

My first thought was to go to the Wizard. He was in Ireland restoring the Glen and its river way, so the leprechauns could return again to Ireland. I found him near the tree where he sleeps at night. He told me that he couldn't leave now because his work was at a critical juncture but he advised me to go back to Never Land and ask the leprechauns for their assistance. "They will know what to do," he said. So, back I went to Never Land. I asked Jenkins what could be done for Dream Walker. He said, "Use all seven of the magic mosses to make a concoction, then force him to swallow it. Chop up all of the mosses very finely, add enough warm water to make a soupy mixture, then spoon it all down Dream Walker's throat." Jenkins gathered the mosses, chopped them very finely and prepared them for me. He handed me a flask of fresh stream water from the magical stream there in Never Land. "Hurry," he told me, "Time is of the essence."

I forced the green goop down Dream Walker's throat. He stirred a little, then awoke and began to share what had happened. He told me that that these creatures were Wararies, and they were tearing apart his dream world. Wararies cook up and consume dreamscapes. I knew then that we needed a lot more than moss to get rid of these bandits. I told Dream Walker to stay away from the Wararies, while I was away finding some way to get rid of them. "I'll be back!" I said. Then I left. I knew too that Dream Walker had depleted all of his energy in the futile effort to sustain his dream world and protect it from these marauders.

I went straight to the Source because this is where the endless supply of energy is located. Last month on the full moon, I received the gift of a magic pearl. It is about the size of a blueberry and has the power to store unlimited amounts of water. I wondered if it might also be able to store energy or light as well. Where the Source resides, there is brilliant white illumination. I removed the magic pearl from its secret pouch and exposed it to the unlimited light, and the unlimited energy. Next I exposed the Other to the same forces, then together, the magical pearl, the Other, and I, went back to the Dream Walkers Realm.

The Other is a luminous double of a sorcerer, which is indestructible and extremely powerful. It cannot be injured and cannot be killed. It is an extension of the sorcerer's will. I am not only a dream walker but also a powerful sorcerer who has created his own double, known as the Other.

The Other entered the cave of the Wararies. There was a brilliant flash of light, and the Wararies came flying out of the cave, never to be seen again. I placed the magical pearl on top of the wooden pole in the large chamber of the cave, which the Wararies had made.

The cave was illuminated in brilliant white light, and an unending stream of water from the magical pearl began to flow. Dream Walker recovered immediately and began moving his personal belongings from his chilly wigwam into the warm cave with its bright light and endless stream of pure spring water.

Heart of Gold

I was visiting my son in Orange County over the weekend. He was getting the pool house ready for expanded use. He asked me if I wanted to stay in the pool house or to stay in the main house in the guest room. I chose to stay in the pool house so I could check it out and make suggestions about what was still needed to make it more functional.

We were also upgrading the pool lighting so it was late when I retired for the evening. Before I went to sleep I checked the place out. There was an Inca warrior standing in the corner of the room by the front door. He was wearing robust looking sandals and a short skirt of some kind. In his left hand he held a short spear upright with its bottom resting on the floor. It was about five feet long. In his right hand he held a small shield about eleven inches wide and twenty inches tall. It was rectangular in shape and was oriented vertically like the spear. On his left wrist he wore a leather bracelet about seven inches wide. He also wore a headband that was ornately decorated with geometric patterns. It was about an inch and one quarter wide and was woven from some kind of white colored plant fibers. On his left arm and shoulder were intricate tattoos. His face had lines tattooed on it. His eyes and the bridge of his nose were also tattooed raccoon-like with an ornate filigreed pattern. I tried to communicate with him several times but he just stood there like a statue not moving a muscle and not responding to my inquiries.

I went out onto the deck near the pool and there stood this Inca Princess with long dark hair clothed in a floor length white robe made of some lite-weight white material. She had been swimming in the pool. I asked her what she was doing there. We were able to communicate but with difficulty. She told me that the Inca warrior was her official personal protector. He traveled everywhere with her. It took some effort but she was finally able to communicate to me that she had been chosen as an Inca princess at an early age and was destined to be sacrificed to the Gods. She had to be a pristine virgin at the time of her sacrifice. The warrior was given the task of protecting her at all times and preserving her purity for the sacrificial offering. She had found her way to me to help her recover her heart that had been ripped out of her chest and offered to the Gods while it was still beating.

The princess then showed me where her heart was located in a vision. It was at the center of some kind of complex matrix where it was still beating keeping the matrix it was connected to functioning. When I told her that I found her entire story to be difficult to believe, she opened her robe revealing a giant hole in her chest where her heart had been ripped out of her body. I told her that I had no idea how I could possible accomplish such a crazy task.

She took my hand and placed it into the hole in her chest and we were all instantly transported back to the time and place where the sacrificial offering was transpiring. The princess was tied on the sacrificial stone. The high priest was standing over her with his flint dagger raised high in the air. His face grimaced. His eyes squinted out from behind raccoon-like tattoos as the sun broke above the distant horizon. I opened the lid of the small domed box and time stood still. I jerked the sacrificial stone dagger from his clinched fists and plunged it deep into his chest cracking several ribs free from their attachments to his sternum. I ripped his beating heart out and placed it into his grasping hands held high above his head. Then, I closed the domed lid of the small box and time resumed. His own heart became the sacrifice to the Gods.

Her personal protector sliced the leather straps restraining the princess and the three of us escaped back into the future as the high priest collapsed still clinging to his own beating heart. My hand was now held against the smooth unblemished skin of the Inca princess' chest. She smiled at me and said, "We traveled all this way to find you because we were told that you were a great sorcerer and could save me from the dreadful death that awaited me. Thank you so much. My protector and I can now share our lives together." They turned and disappeared together into a dense jungle setting somewhere in their past. I was left standing alone in front of the pool house at my son's house in Orange County, contemplating what had just transpired.

Itsacono

Sharing this experience is intended only to expand the arena of possibility for you. I was awake and in bed when images about six inches square began to appear in my field of vision. These images were the same with my eyes open or with them closed. An image would form then some parts of it would animate and then that image would be replaced by another image emerging from the right side of my field of vision and exiting to the left side of my field of vision. It was almost like a slide show. This process continued for a long time. I was trying to figure out how this process was possible. The images appeared to be elaborate etchings or engravings to be used to illustrate books or papers from a long time ago before there were any photographs available. The content appeared to be from the fourteenth or fifteenth century based on the subjects and the subject matter. I don't know what they were supposed to refer to. While focused on this process a scene from a dense jungle momentarily appeared. Between the leaves I saw part of a face staring out at me. It was the left eye and cheek of a person. I noticed the glint in the eye as well as the white sclera when the eye moved. It appeared to me to be the face of an Inca Indian. Their faces are unique. I didn't know for sure if it were the face of a female or of a younger male but I was determined to find that person.

It took a while but I located him in the jungle deep in the past. I presented myself in a small clearing in the jungle as an Aborigine dressed only in a leather thong given to me by Aru the keeper of Dream Time. As he circled around me I moved to face him as though I were standing on a turntable. Communication was clear and precise though neither he nor I moved our lips. Communication must have been telepathic. He told me that his mother's dying wish was for him to find the Sorcerer who had rescued her and his warrior father from certain death.

I asked if she were still alive. He said that she was. He took me to her. She was lying in her bed waiting for death to take her. She had cataracts and was blind. I magically removed her cataracts and she could see once again but she didn't recognize me in my present form as an Aborigine. I told her that I was a shape shifter and transformed myself back into a familiar form. Because she could now see once again she resumed her daily activities and I departed back into my own time.

I asked the Source how that whole process could have transpired and how the Inca Prince could have located me far in the future. He said that we must have some history. We must have some connection. I wondered if he possibly could have been a prior incarnation of myself. To test this hypothesis I went to the edge of the abyss and crossed over on the 'Wizard's Bridge.' On the other side of the abyss standing on the right side of that end of the bridge are all of my former incarnations. The Inca Prince was there among them. He was a former incarnation of myself. The Source told me some time ago that I must locate each of my past and future incarnations and meld with them before I would be complete. I put the Inca Prince on like you would put on a Hawaiian shirt and then went through the 'Door of No Return' and we were one. I had gone back in time and saved the Inca Princess and her warrior guard who became the parents of the Inca Prince who summoned me from the future at his mother's request. Itsacono the Inca prince is a prior incarnation of myself.

Ligot

Ligot is a word I encountered a few days ago. I am not sure what it is exactly. I have a vague idea based on the context in which the word was used. I don't know if it is a thing or a concept or a belief or exactly what but I think it is worth the effort to try to find out. It occurred to me that whatever ligot turns out to be, it might possibly have some connection with the anger Phillip is struggling with.

I asked the Source if he would tell me anything about the term ligot even though I was quite sure that he wouldn't do so. Like usual I was going to be on my own in dealing with this challenge.

After many unsuccessful attempts to get at the meaning of the word ligot I decided to go to Vishnu's Island to see if anyone there could provide me with some insight. I situated myself in front of the fire pit with its smoldering embers. First I Invited Hanuman the Monkey God to come to the fire pit, which was our usual gathering place. I asked Hanuman if he knew anything about ligot, then proceeded to describe ligot, as I understood its nature. Hanuman said that he had never heard of ligot and was adamant that a thing like that would be a warrior's greatest enemy, for emotions could never be allowed to enter into mortal combat.

Next I invited Shiva the destroyer, the God of Destruction to come. He arrived in short order but he too said that he had never heard of such a word. He stated that the goal of destroying anything was always in preparation for creating something new that would replace what has been destroyed. I knew that Ganesh worked in concert with Shiva to create the new to replace the old so it was unlikely that he would know anything that Shiva did not already know.

The next God I invited to come to the fire pit was Krishna. He always provides me with valuable insight into my inquiries. Krishna said that ligot was not a demon or a god but actually a state of mind that developed in the unsophisticated minds of jungle tribesmen when they were confronted with primal fear of the unknown and great loss because they lacked the coping strategies that better educated people have at their disposal. He suggested that I seek advice from the Buddha. So I did. When the Buddha arrived, he said to me, "You look familiar. I think our paths have crossed before." I told him that I was a traveler and that I have been in many different places at many different times. I asked him about the word ligot and asked what information he could give me concerning it.

The Buddha said, "Ligot is the response of uncontrollable rage that arises from within primitive minds of jungle tribesmen when they encounter a tragic loss combined with the extreme fear of the unknown. All human suffering has its origins in their attachments to things and their attachments to their beliefs, for nothing is permanent. All things pass away. True bliss lies in living in the moment for the past has gone and the future never comes. Only this moment is real. We will meet again when our paths cross." Then he was gone.

Chief Red Shirt

By thy hand I thus inscribe –
Violence begets violence.
Tis true – tis true, as any man can speak.
Show not thy violent side in speech nor deed.
Surely time will bless thee as none other.
But, cousin to crow and engine of life,
these gifts be tools when wisely spent,
not in violence gainst thy brother,
but in love, patience and fortitude.
These words come from my song,
from song of life and longing for peace,
for all, men and not.
This gift of peace I pass to you.
Kill no other.
Save thyself and brother –
for all time.

Chief Red Shirt

Little Bear

Yesterday morning I took the trash from the kitchen
out to the alley behind our house and tossed it into the
large, green, communal trash container. On my way

back I noticed that someone had trimmed the grass around our water-meter box and raked the cuttings into a circle about three-feet in diameter around the meter-cover. I have never seen that done before and we have lived in this house forty-five years. About two feet away from the water-meter is a large pine-tree with a trunk about eighteen inches in diameter.

Last night while I was talking with the Source, my visual field was suddenly filled with the water-meter scene and the large pine-tree trunk. Just behind the meter-cover and next to the pine-tree I saw the snout of a small brown bear. I got down on my hands and knees and crawled over to where the small bear was hiding. It turned and moved back into the shadows. I scurried after it and found myself in the middle of the prairie in thick buffalo grass. There standing in front of me was a young Indian boy about ten years of age. I recognized him as the boy that I have had other adventures with in the past. He was wearing deerskin jerkins and moccasins. He had long, dark, hair tied neatly back in a ponytail and he was shirtless. I assumed that I was also a young boy like I had been in other adventures with him. On one previous occasion I had been an Indian boy and on another occasion I had been an Anglo. I looked at my hands. They were bear-paws, covered in thick, brown fur.

As we stood there in the tall prairie grass, the boy grew older and became a young man then an older man and finally he became a chief wearing a full, feathered headdress. At that point he sat down in a small circular clearing in front of a fire-pit with rocks around it. He lit a fire then put dry grass into the fire until smoke began billowing up into the sky. I climbed into the smoke as it rose slowly upwards and I became a man once again. The Indian Chief climbed up into the smoke after me. As he climbed inside the smoke he was transformed into a bear. I asked him what his name was and he said, "Little Bear." I asked the bear what my name was and he said, "Traveler…You are the traveler."

We talked briefly about the nature and purpose of the smoke. He told me that to an Indian, smoke reveals the true nature and form of everything. Then, I asked him who he actually was. He said that he was "Little Bear" and that this was his true form. He was a bear. Then I asked him who I was and he said, "You are 'Druid,' I am 'Little Bear.'"

Coyote's Howl

It was September 24th, the night of the Harvest Moon. It was after midnight. I was talking with the Source. As we walked along in the light from the full moon he said to me that he was giving me the 'Gift of Life.' I heard a coyote's mournful howl in the distance. I was very excited to receive the 'Gift of Life.' What a magnificent gift to share with others. He then told me that with the 'Gift of Life' came the 'Curse of Death.' I was very distraught because that was the last thing I wanted to have. I told the Source that I could never be trusted with the 'Curse of Death,' for surely I would begin killing all of those I felt were justly deserving of such a fate. The Source elaborated, "There is no good without evil. There is no Yin without Yang." He said that I must decide for he would not again offer to bestow this 'Gift of Life' upon me. I didn't know what to do. What a magnificent gift... What a horrible curse.

The coyote howled three times. It was closer now. I went to visit the coyote and shape-shifted myself into a coyote and sat down in front of it in the moonlight. I shared my dilemma with the Wise and Wiley coyote. He said that I must accept the gift that was offered to me. When I complained about the curse that accompanied this gift. He said, "A dog without a bite is all bark, and not a real dog at all." I returned and informed the Source that I would accept the "Gift of Life" The coyote howled three times. The Source then gave me the 'Curse of Death." The coyote howled six times and my Fate was sealed. I asked the Source if the gift of life could be bestowed upon another person from a distance. He said that the 'Gift of Life' could only be transferred by touch because life is a physical state but the 'Curse of Death' could be delivered by coming out from within the dreamscape like Freddy Kruger, for death is a non-physical state.

A couple of hours later, I heard the coyote howl mournfully in the distance. My wife began to shake and gasp for breath in her sleep. I was afraid she might be dying. I touched her. I shared the 'Gift of Life' with her and she returned to a peaceful state of sleep. In the distance, the coyote howled twice with seeming satisfaction.

In the morning, my wife shared a strange dream she had during the night. She said that she was at a gathering where two of her great uncles greeted her happily with hugs and adulation. She asked them if they knew who she was, for she had not seen them since she was a young girl. They said of course they knew who she was. There were several other people gathered there as well. All of them now long since dead and buried.

The Pasture

Last night the Source took me to a place he called the "Pasture." He asked me to tell him what I saw. I have never seen anything that was remotely similar to what I was observing. There was an expansive flat space where there were vertical striations emitting from the ground. They were narrow, all different in color, in pattern and in frequency of vibration. The colors were not brilliant but subdued. I had no idea what these things were. I knew the Source was pushing me to go beyond any self-imposed limitations.

I summoned the wizard's powers of observation and this is what I saw:

The striations disappeared and out of the dusky background emerged an Indian, bare-chested in long leather jerkins and simple moccasins. His hair was long, dark and braided and there was one feather canted off to one side. I recognized him at first sight as the spirit shape shifting coyote. He stopped and stood all the way to the left side and became the coyote. Next came the spirit deer, then the bear, the wolf, the hawk, the eagle, the elk, the skunk, the raccoon, one by one until all the spirit animals of Indian myth and religion had emerged and shape shifted into their spirit animal form. I went out to meet them.

One by one I shape shifted into each of the different animals and greeted them as brothers. When that process was completed they all vanished and the "Pasture" became an inland expanse of water. One by one it populated with all of the spirit creatures of the lakes and rivers and sea. When all of the water spirits were assembled I greeted them individually and shape shifted into their animal forms. After I greeted each and all, everything disappeared and I was standing alone next to the Source in an expansive verdant alpine meadow ringed with pine and fir and white aspen. The Source asked me if I understood what I had just experienced. My answer:

"How do I get people to understand?"

Apache Junction

Last night when I was talking with the Source I asked him what was next on his agenda for me to do. He said that he wanted me to go to Apache Junction.

When I was young we would drive through Apache Junction on our way to the lakes and trout streams in northern Arizona. There were two roads that crossed in the middle of the desert. That was Apache Junction. When I was little, I don't think there were even any stop signs just one road going north intersecting one road going east and west. When I was in college the roads were paved, had two lanes and a couple of stop signs that was it, no gas station, no houses, no people, only two roads crossing in the middle of no where. I could not even imagine what I was supposed to accomplish by going to Apache Junction.

When I got there they were having a pow-wow. There were lots of Indians everywhere. Some were decked out in traditional attire some were not. There were traditional drums and dancing as well as modern dancing and music. There was fry-bread and traditional as well as fast food concessions. There were pickups everywhere. They were mostly white Ford and Chevy models.

There was only one traditional tee-pee situated off to one edge of the pow-wow, with smoke trailing up out of the top opening where the supporting poles crossed and the flaps were pulled back for ventilation. I poked my head inside. There was total silence. Outside it was extremely noisy, inside not a single sound. One Indian man sat in front of the fire-pit located in the center of the tent dressed in a light tan buckskin outfit. His legs were crossed. He had a single eagle feather sticking straight up out of his headband. His long braided hair fell to one side of his weathered face. I assumed that he was a medicine man. I didn't stay long inside before I went back outside where the music was playing and there was food and dancing going on everywhere.

When I got back home I wondered what the point of going to Apache Junction had been. It couldn't have been for the music or the food or even the dancing. It must have had something to do with the medicine man in the tee-pee filled with its strange silence. So, I went back to the pow-wow in Apache Junction and back into that tee-pee. I sat down in front of the fire pit directly across from the medicine man facing him. He took out his medicine pipe and lit it. He puffed on it several times and blew smoke over onto me. The smoke felt like acid eating away at my skin. I looked down at my body and I was a giant tooth being etched by acid before a new crown is placed down over it. I got up and left as fast as I could and returned home. The burning sensation subsided and I gave the whole experience some more thought. I still had no idea what the point of the experience had been but I knew that I needed to go back to Apache Junction again to try to find out.

When I returned to the pow-wow the medicine man was still sitting cross leg in front of the fire pit. I sat down directly across from him as he took out his medicine pipe again and began to puff on it. A large cloud of smoke billowed upwards in front of him and formed an Indian deer dancer that was in full costume complete with antlers and head mask. Then he handed his pipe to me.

I took the pipe from him in the traditional manner and began to puff on it. The smoke billowed up above the fire pit and became a great bear, a grizzly bear. The Indian deer dancer slowly dissipated and vanished into thin air but the grizzly bear became more and more real. It descended down upon me and I was transformed into a giant grizzly bear. The medicine man told me that I was to walk the earth from now on as a grizzly bear. For Native Americans the great grizzly bear has always been their spiritual protector here on earth.

I now understood what the importance was for me to go to Apache Junction. It is clear now what my future will be.

When I mentioned this to the Source he said, "All my children are turning away from the light. Guide them back from darkness."

Goose-Bay Crossing

I was awake in time to catch the Night Bus that would be coming by at 2:00 o'clock in the morning. I had no idea where to go but the name Goose Bay Crossing popped into my head. I didn't know where Goose Bay Crossing was but it sounded like it would probably be cold and wet wherever it might be, so I put on my light-blue full-length parka, my new hat with the ear flaps pulled down, my warmest gloves and my heavy leather boots with two pair of socks for good measure. I stuffed my pockets with matches, a flashlight, a compass, a bottle of water, a handkerchief for my nose which would probably be dripping from the cold air and last but not least a peanut butter and peach-jam sandwich. Then, I trudged out and waited under the street lamp in front of my driveway for the Night Bus to come. As usual, it arrived right on time.

When the bus stopped and the door swung open on the antique old bus, I hopped on and told Brad Coon the driver, "Goose Bay Crossing!" His eyes got big and his mouth fell open showing all those pointy raccoon teeth and he exclaimed, "Goose Bay Crossing?" I said, "Yes" and we were off on another adventure.

Brad coaxed the old bus into the intersection. Then he turned it around so we were now heading in the opposite direction and floored it. We gathered speed faster and faster as we headed for the end of my street that ended in a 'T' with no way forward but only ninety degree turns to the right and to the left. We were headed straight for a cement-block wall at breakneck speed.

At the last second, instead of smashing into that wall, we entered 'Super Slow Motion' and went through a curtain of yellow Jell-O. When we came out the other side, we were floating through the air in near darkness. We floated down and came to a gentle landing on a sand bar in the middle of a bay surrounded on all sides by water. As I hopped off of the bottom step, Brad saluted me and the Night Bus was gone. I was left standing on one foot on the sand bar that protruded just a few inches above the water on the smooth surface of the bay.

The night sky was alive with dancing iridescent streams of northern lights from the Aurora Borealis. As my eyes scanned the panoramic twilight horizon my head seemed to be on a swivel, because I could survey it in a complete circle. When I looked down at the single foot I was standing on, it was a big black, duck-foot attached to a spindly, black, bird-leg. I looked at my chest. It was completely covered with gray feathers. The dim reflection from the surface of the water confirmed my suspicion. I was a Canadian Gray Goose, dressed in its feathered splendor. I spread my arms. They were magnificent gray wings.

I was there alone in the winter twilight standing on one foot on a small sand bar in the middle of the bay, somewhere in Canada, at Goose Bay Crossing. I tucked my head under my wing. I was snug and warm and safe from the whistling wind and freezing waters with my head nestled in the softest, warmest, goose-down pillow you could ever imagine, waiting for long winter's twilight to be broken once again by the return of the sun and the coming of spring. Then, once again, I would go fishing and dancing on the glassy smooth waters of 'Goose Bay Crossing.'

Big Daddy

Last night at 12:37, my wife woke me up complaining that something had whacked the side of the bed, real hard. I said I would check it out and take care of whatever it was. At the corner of the bed on her side was a huge octopus. I asked it, if it really were an octopus. The octopus said that yes, it was in fact, an octopus. "This is the middle of the desert. How can an octopus be in the middle of the desert in my bedroom?" I asked. The octopus told me that this was actually the middle of the ocean and what was this bed doing in the middle of the ocean? In total disbelief, I got my rose-colored glasses and put them on. Sure enough, we were in the middle of a turbulent ocean with dark angry clouds and waves crashing all around. And sure enough there was a very large octopus there at the foot of the bed.

He told me that his name was 'Big Daddy' and this was the ocean of sorrows. As I continued with my questions, he told me that they call him Big Daddy because his tentacles spread out more than twelve feet across, from tip to tip. He said that the Ocean of Sorrows had no bottom and had no edges. This didn't sound very encouraging. I was noticing how the bed had been slowly sinking into the ocean further and further with each passing moment. I was racking my brain for some strategy on how to extricate myself and my wife, and hopefully our bed, from this dilemma, while she snored away.

Then the thought occurred to me that what I needed was just the opposite of sinking into the ocean. I needed to be rising up out of the Ocean of Sorrows, and what was the opposite of sorrow? It was joy. So, I started enumerating each and everything in my life that truly gives me joy. As I did so, in a very loud voice, the bed began to rise further and further until it was completely out of the water and the clouds began to dissipate and the ocean grew calm. The more I acknowledged these things the faster we moved upwards into the sky and a beautiful sunset appeared. I headed home and soon found myself back in our bedroom with all three of us there, my wife, our bed, and I.

A little while later, my wife awoke and said "Rabbit." I returned the, "Rabbit." The first one to wake up after midnight on the first day of each new month says, "Rabbit." We believe that brings us good luck for the coming month.

She went back to sleep and I went in search of answers as to why that scenario had transpired. I was told that the events of the evening were created by:

1) My recent gift of understanding combined with,
2) All Souls Day (what we celebrate here as Dia De Los Muertos), which started at midnight and
3) All of the sorrows of all those who have died that created the Ocean of Sorrows, which knows no boundaries, and has no bottom.

The Tiger in the Tree

It was 2:00 o'clock when I woke up this morning and checked the clock. I leaped out of bed and ran out to the curb by the street in front of our house. The night bus screeched to a stop. I jumped through the open door and yelled to the driver, "Take me on an adventure." He slammed the door shut and goosed the old bus with both hands firmly on the steering wheel. We weaved in and out of invisible traffic, then we entered a dark tunnel. The bus did a few barrel rolls on the inside of the tunnel before we finally came to an abrupt stop. The driver shoved the lever hard and the door sprang open. He shouted out, "Adventure Land."

I jumped from the top step and landed in the middle of a tropical jungle. The Night Bus instantly disappeared and I was alone. I looked down. My skin was black. I had no shoes, shirt or pants, only a thong. Never ask a wily raccoon to take you on an adventure. You might end up in the middle of the jungle wearing nothing but a thong.

This jungle was really dense. I couldn't see two feet in front of me. I climbed the largest tree I could find to get the lay of the land. The canopy of trees stretched endlessly as far as I could see in every direction. There were no mountains or hills or breaks in the dense forest. The low-hanging clouds covered the sun. It was impossible to tell one direction from another. I knew then that this was going to be 'no cakewalk.' I had to come up with a viable security strategy and fast. In the city I might be a top predator but in the jungle I was certain to be on someone's menu.

The top predator in this jungle was the Bengal Tiger. A bent stick or a sharp rock was no match for a hungry carnivore. I needed to make friends with a tiger and fast. I came across an animal trail and followed it until I encountered a hungry tigress munching on the remains of a large deer. She growled menacingly but continued with her meal. I sat down on the ground as close to her as she would allow. Every time she looked away I inched closer and closer, until I was finally right next to the deer's head. When she was completely stuffed she crept back into the forest. I sat there unmoving until she returned the next day to finish her meal. She growled intermittently as she polished off the rest of the deer. I never moved and I never touched her deer.

I followed her at a distance until she climbed up into a towering tree with huge branches protruding out horizontally from its trunk. She climbed up on the largest branch and stretched out on it with all four legs hanging down. When she dozed off I climbed up onto an adjacent branch and stretched out on it with my arms and legs hanging down, like her, where we could keep an eye on each other. I awoke later and discovered that she was gone. That evening she returned dragging a dead pig. Before she could even get a single bite, an even larger male tiger challenged her for her pig.

I knew that if the tigress lost her pig or was chased away by the larger more aggressive male tiger, I would probably be his next meal. I felt compelled to help my potential benefactor, so I jumped out of the tree onto the back of the unsuspecting tiger far below. I landed with such great force that he was knocked flat. I grabbed him around the neck in a chokehold and latched onto his ear with my teeth as he ran into the jungle. I knew if I let go I would certainly be his dinner. It was a wild ride but he eventually passed out as I chewed a piece of his ear off. I returned to the tigress and her pig, spit the ear out in front of her and returned to my branch above as 'The Tiger in the Tree.'

The Hounds of Baskerville

Yesterday morning at a little after 4:30 a.m., my wife rolled over and said to me, "There's something here." That is always a request, not a statement. She always wants to know what the story is, as well as what is actually there.

There was nothing beside the bed but stretched across the open door to our bedroom was what appeared to be this large, gray, animal skin. It looked like a really big wolf skin. The snout was attached at the top of the lintel, in the center. The front paws stretched out horizontally and were attached over the sides of the doorjamb, while the two back legs were attached at the bottom corners. On the other side of the doorway, in the hall, were a bunch of big black dogs with brown muzzles that were barking and jumping around, trying to get past the outstretched gray wolf skin.

I never panic. I always follow a protocol. "Who are you? What do you want? Why are you here? What are those dogs doing jumping around in the hallway?" I was somewhat surprised that answers came quite quickly …telepathically.

From what I thought was an animal skin came the emphatic answer that she was the Gray Wolf of the North and she was keeping the Hounds of Baskerville at bay.

I got out of bed and went to the doorway, stuck my head around the big gray wolf and yelled at the hound dogs, "Get lost." In great surprise, they all froze with wide eyes and mouths falling open, turned quickly on their heels and dashed down the hall and out through the walls of the house. There appeared to be three or four of them, but in the darkened hallway, there may have been even more.

I invited the Gray Wolf of the North to come over to

my side of the bed. She released her jaws clamped to the doorjamb, dropped to the floor, and moved close to me beside the bed and sat down on her haunches. She was huge, far larger than any wolf I had ever seen. As I continued asking her one question after another, she provided me with strange and implausible answers.

She told me that her name was Tinian and she had come to the rescue because the Hounds of Baskerville were chasing my Cardigan Welsh Corgi. I asked the she wolf, how could that be, my dog was asleep in his bed, there in our bedroom.

Her answer was that my dog was dreaming and the hounds began chasing him in his dream. The problem was that the walls of our house are riddled with holes and tunnels and portals and passageways from all of the many years of me traveling through them on my endless adventures in search of the 'Holy Grail.' That allowed the Hounds of Baskerville to fly right out of the dreamscape and right into our house. They would have gotten to my dog, the she wolf said, if it were not for her swift and decisive intervention.

I never pass up an opportunity to inquire, no matter how bizarre a situation might be, as to the acquisition of logical ancillary information. So, I asked, if she were the Gray Wolf of the North, were there possibly… other cardinal wolves as well. She said, "Yes there is the Wolf of the South, the Wolf of the West and also the Wolf of the East."

This sounded like an opportunity to me, worthy of further investigation.

The Four Cardinal Wolves

Last night I summoned the four wolves one by one until all four of them were present together. First of all, I wanted to find out if there really were other wolves besides the Gray Wolf of the North, and secondly, I wanted to have some idea what they might be capable of doing.

The first one of the wolves that I summoned was naturally, the Gray Wolf of the North because we had already met the night before, and she had demonstrated an impressive capacity to communicate clearly, which in and of itself could prove to be an invaluable asset.

The second wolf I summoned was logically the Wolf of the South. This wolf turned out to be a jet-black male whose name was Buschard. Next I summoned the Wolf of the East. This wolf was a snow white female with the name Estrella. The last wolf, the Wolf of the West, was a red wolf, whose name was Willis. That left me with four giant wolves, Tinian, Buschard, Estrella, & Willis.

When I put on the rose-colored glasses and looked at each of the wolves, their appearance changed. The white wolf became a single red rose. The black wolf turned into a white chrysanthemum. The red wolf was a red tulip and the gray wolf became a white jonquil. Next, I warned the four wolves that I would draw my trusty sword before I did, so they would have no reason to bolt at the sight of it. When I drew the sword and stared into its reflective surface, each of the wolves became a shade, a bizarre wispy creature associated with death and dying that comes straight from the underworld.

I remembered the golden disc that I wear on a gold chain around my neck at all times. It was a gift from Osiris, the Egyptian God of the Underworld. It has deep and permanent magic. It is a little more than six inches in diameter with a smooth lustrous surface, about one inch thick in the center and tapers off in a gentle curve towards its rounded edges. This disc emits the light of the full moon. It also provides me with clear passage through the underworld and protects me from any harm that originates in the underworld. It was indispensable during my many excursions into the realm of the dead.

As I cast the moonlight emitted from the glowing disc onto each shade, it disintegrated into a fine powder that fell to the ground forming a small conical pile. After the last shade disintegrated, I once again observed each wolf through the rose-colored glasses. Each individual flower was transformed into a large bouquet of flowers, a bouquet of red roses, one of white chrysanthemums, another of colorful red tulips and another of white jonquils.

I removed the glasses and once again there were four wolves staring at me in amazement. They began frolicking around, jumping, barking and playing together as only canines can. They couldn't believe that they were free at last, free to be free, no longer tethered to the shades of the underworld. They were free to be what they were, agents of change. The four Cardinal Wolves, four agents of change, magical creatures capable of creating change in your life, in my life, in everyone's lives. They ran into the meadow and it burst into a colorful display of endless spring flowers of every kind and color. Then each disappeared over the hill into their cardinal direction, leaving me alone in an endless field of flowers.

Stone Dragon & Fetch

I was in the 'dream scape' last night walking in a desert arroyo when I passed a sentry-dog on the other side of a metal gate. The gate was not connected to a fence, just a driveway size Cyclone gate with no fence on either side. The dog was a large German shepherd police dog. It was running back and forth on the other side of the gate, barking like crazy. I was sure it was going to attack me. I wrapped my handkerchief around the knuckles on my right hand in preparation for a fight that I knew was imminent. The dog ran around the right end of the gate and came at me full speed.

As I crouched and turned to face him, he sailed right past me and ran straight to a large boulder about twenty feet away in the middle of the arroyo. He jumped against the boulder with his front paws and the rock was transformed into a 'Stone Dragon,' not a fire-breathing dragon with wings but it was more like a very large, fat alligator with long legs. The dog sat down next to the stone dragon, stared at me, panting with his tongue lolling out from all his exertion. I had no idea what was going on. So I decided that I needed to ask the dragon.

I sat down directly in front of the stone dragon that was now moving his head all about. When I asked who he was and who the dog was and what the point was of this whole experience, the dragon told me that he was the 'Stone Dragon' and the German shepherd was named 'Fetch.' He said that whenever I was at a loss for a word to describe something exactly the way it should be described I should ask Fetch and he would come to the stone in the arroyo and jump up on it and the 'Stone Dragon' would emerge from the rock and give Fetch that perfect word I was looking for and Fetch would bring the perfect word back to me so that I could describe it perfectly. The police dog fetches whatever word I need from the Stone Dragon. That is why he is called 'Fetch.'

Monster Mash

A couple of days ago the Source told me that it was time for me to be exposed to the 'Monster Mash.' He didn't elaborate or explain any further as to what the Monster Mash was or how I should get there. He felt that I was ready now to go there on my own.

First I tried going on the 'Night Bus' but that didn't work out so well. The next night I tried taking the 'Night Train' and that didn't go so well either. Last night I tried again for the third time by first locating the doorway to 'Monster Mash.' Then, I proceeded to enter through the door marked 'Monster Mash.'

The door itself was not that unusual but it was actually thicker and heavier than an ordinary door. It was made of solid wood more than two inches thick. Most doors are less than two inches thick. The upper half had frosted glass in it but the glass itself was almost half an inch thick. The words, MONSTER MASH, were stenciled onto the thick security glass in large upper-case black letters. The surface of the glass was not smooth but textured and bumpy. The door opened outward hung in a solid rock wall revealing a tunnel through solid stone with straight vertical walls, a flat floor and an arched ceiling. The tunnel was a little over seven feet long and seven feet wide. The highest point on the arch was a little less than eight feet. This tunnel opened into another world filled with all sorts of monsters of different sizes, shapes and colors. The monsters were all bipedal and reminiscent of dinosaurs that walked on two legs.

The monsters were all moving around aimlessly ignoring each other and me as well. In an effort to better understand what they were and what the point of me being there was, I first observed them through the rose-colored glasses. That made them all more colorful. Then I looked at them through the double-lensed pince-nez spectacles. They then appeared to all be small rodent size monsters. With the reflection from the magic sword they all appeared as different colored monster mice. Finally with the use of the rose-colored glasses along with the double-lensed pince-nez spectacles and the reflection from the sword of truth, they all appeared as small mice all wearing different colored clothing walking around upright on their hind legs.

None of this made any sense to me until I witnessed them interacting with each other. They were all small talking mice. They completely ignored each other unless they were interacting with another mouse attempting to get something from the other mouse. All of their interaction was through flattery and deceit.

Then I understood that 'Monster Mash' was an allegory of how we humans run around ignoring everyone else, unless we are trying to get something from them through our flattery and lies.

We are all monsters and our interactions with each other, is the, 'Monster Mash.'

When I discussed this with the Source he was pleased that I understood what the lesson actually was. I asked him if I were still a wizardling or was I now a wizard. His only comment was, "You're getting there...you are getting there."

Deming

This morning, at 2:00 o'clock I went out to the street in front of our house to see if anything was going on. There was a stagecoach stopped right in front of our driveway. I climbed on board and the coach began moving. It was bouncing along down a rutted dusty road not much more than a trail barely wide enough for a horse-drawn wagon.

Sitting directly across facing me was a cowboy with a long mustache who could have used a bath and a shave. He said. " Where ya headed, pardner?" No body in their right mind goes to Deming so I said, "El Paso."

I said. "And you?" He replied, "Durango." We bounced along in silence. I put my head back and pulled my Stetson hat down over my eyes like I was sleeping. Sitting next to me on my left side was a nicely dressed young lady maybe in her thirties. Before long I felt those delicate hands checking my pockets for any loose cash or a watch and my belt for a hidden purse.

I reached down slowly with my right hand and pulled my Colt 380 automatic that I always carry, out of my boot and the delicate little hands vanished. The cowboy retorted, "What is that? I've never seen nuttin like that in my life!"

I dropped the clip into my lap with a flick of my thumb, pulled the slide, opened the breach and handed it to the cowboy butt-first without lifting my hat off

70

from over my eyes. He was totally in shock for nothing like that would be invented in his lifetime.

The stagecoach came rumbling to a halt. The driver yelled out "Deming." I got up and said, "This is my stop."

The shocked cowboy blurted out, "Where you from, pardner?"

I smiled and said, as I relieved him of my semi-automatic 380 Colt pistol, "The future... The future." And, I got down from the stagecoach we were riding in.

There was not much more than a saloon and a livery stable in Deming. I made my way into the saloon and sat dawn at the bar put my automatic pistol on the counter in front of me and ordered a drink with my two fingers. The patrons stared at me in my clean suit and new red boots. They all thought I was a gambler for sure. The bartender said twenty-five cents. I chugged the two fingers of whisky and smacked down a shiny two thousand and seventeen quarter and got up to leave. The bartender said, "Where you from man?"

I replied, " The future man... The future" and I disappeared.

Deming is a town in New Mexico located in Luna County thirty-three miles north of Mexico and sixty miles west of Las Cruces. In 1850 it was a Butterfield Stage stop.

Lone Rider

Early this morning when I returned to bed after going to the bathroom, the red numbers displayed on the face of the clock glowed 3:44. I decided to go outside in front of our house to see if anything was coming. Everything looked normal. The LED street lamp was illuminated. The street was completely empty of cars or people and the curb was still there, as well as the familiar cracked asphalt with its pocked-marked face awaiting its long overdue repairs. At 3:45 I turned around to go back to the house when I heard a clacking sound in the distance at the far end of our street. There, under that street lamp was a cowboy riding his horse slowly towards me. His head was hung over so far down on his chest he appeared to be the headless-horseman. I went back out into the middle of the street and awaited their arrival. The horse was very tall as was the cowboy in his faded and badly worn attire. The horse had its head hung over too, as it plodded along very slowly coming closer and closer towards me. I reached out with my left arm fully extended and put the palm of my hand on the nose of the horse. It stopped in its tracks and stared at me through glassy eyes. Some kind of energy passed through my arm and into my body. I was transformed into an old cowboy myself with dusty faded boots and crusty sunbaked skin, a faded leather vest and a long gray beard.

This aroused the sleeping cowboy with his badly weathered hat pulled down low over his eyes. His head came slowly up from his chest and he appraised me with glowing red eyes as though he were the devil himself. He drew his pearl-handled six-gun with his right hand, pointed it straight at me, then twirled it around his trigger finger three times before slamming it back into its holster. He wrapped the reins around the saddle horn, drew his other pistol with his left hand and repeated this process of pointing it straight at my face twirling it around his trigger finger, then re-holstering it. The devil-eyed cowboy turned his horse slowly around with a flip of its reins, then they departed slowly back down the street from whence they came.

That was the weirdest thing ever. I asked everyone I could think of for a possible explanation. No one had any ideas. Finally I asked the Source. The Source knows all but seldom shares information until after I have exhausted all other possibilities. Even this explanation left me with many unanswered questions. The Source said that I had just met myself. The Source told me that this cowboy was born in 1810 and it was the 1850's when we met. I was transformed into the old cowboy that he would become at my age, the age of seventy-two. He was in his mid-forties. He recognized me as himself, as the old bearded man he would someday become and he left me in peace.

At 4:43, I ventured back out into the street in front of our house out of curiosity. As I turned to go back inside at 4:44, a glint of steel reflected from that same street lamp at the far end of our street caught my eye. It came from the polished armor of a jousting knight. His lance was pointed straight at me as he cantered his powerful armored horse straight down the street towards me. Just before his lance reached me he reigned in his steed, raised his lance slightly, then lowered it gently onto my left shoulder and saluted with a quick snap of his left arm straight across his chest. He whirled his horse around and they galloped away at full speed, back into the past from where they had come.

At 5:20, I again stood in the street facing that same street lamp. A Roman foot soldier with short sword drawn, shield in hand, helmeted and covered in breastplate and skirted armor, steadily approached. I departed before being killed by my own hand.

Six Guns

Early this morning before 1:00 o'clock I went outside to the driveway and stood under the street lamp to see if the night plane would be passing by. Nothing was happening so I sat down on the edge of the street and waited. I was anticipating the sound of some kind of airplane approaching in the distance. Instead I heard the unmistakable clop, clop clopping of a horse's hoofs on the hard asphalt surface of the road.

The horse stopped near by me. When I looked up the rider had dismounted and whipped out both of his pistols as he appeared from behind his horse. He stood directly in front of me with both of his guns pointed straight at my forehead. I recognized this cowboy from an encounter two years ago on this same street right in front of my house. He was a past incarnation of myself. He was the "Lone Rider" from the first book of the trilogy, "Coincidental Journey."

The Lone Rider spun the pistols backwards on his trigger fingers then slapped them down on the ground in front of me with their barrels pointed directly at me. Without speaking a single word he remounted his steed and whorled his horse around and they slowly plodded back down the road the way they had come. I watched them as they moved towards the 'T' intersection at the end of our street. As they entered the intersection they vanished into a shimmering mirage. I picked up the two pistols and spun them deftly backwards around my trigger fingers. They felt like extensions of my own hands, as though I had done it before a thousand times. They were a matched pair of pearl-handled Colt long-barrel 44's. I took them into the house with me and placed them gingerly on the floor next to my nightstand. I asked the Source what the whole encounter was really all about. He told me that I should take them with me where ever I traveled because I would need them to protect myself. He also reminded me of the necessity of establishing contact with all of my past incarnations. This can most readily be accomplished by crossing over ”The Wizard's Bridge” and onto the other side of the "Abyss."

Spectrum

One night in the past, when I checked in with the Source, he began walking and wanted to re-visit the topic of fog and smoke. He reminded me that fog and smoke were created by un-certainty. He then pointed out the absence of fog and smoke as we walked towards the abyss. "You have obviously devised a way to manage uncertainty effectively," he said. "You are ready now to see the Spectrum. In front of you is the abyss. You can see the edge where what we are walking on meets the abyss. To the right is the Place of Emptiness. To the left is the Void. If you put your hand into the Place of Emptiness it will disappear, for there is nothing physical in the Place of Emptiness. If you put your hand into the Void, your hand will still exist and your spectrum will also exist, there in that 'Void.'

A spectrum appeared like a giant rainbow in the void. The Source said, "The spectrum is a reflection of indifference, your indifference. It appears as your spectrum in the Void." The spectrum that appeared in front of me from within the abyss was absent many of its bars of color. It was incomplete.

"Your task is to complete the spectrum and fill the

blank spaces with their missing colors. Then you will no longer bear the burden of indifference." The Source disappeared leaving me alone to contemplate on how to abandon my personal indifferences and to thereby restore my spectrum in its entirety.

That encounter happened quite some time ago. Last night I returned to the 'Wizards Bridge.' I crossed over the bridge and on the other side I met up with many of my past lives. We formed a circle and merged into a singularity. My spectrum re-appeared. It was now almost complete. Apparently this technique is effective in compensating for my own personal indifferences.

Miazon

The next night I went back out to the street at 1:41 in the morning to see if any other strange characters would arrive from somewhere in my past. At the end of the street under the streetlight an Asian looking man dressed in a full-length white, goat-wool robe of a pale bluish-gray tint appeared, seemingly out of thin air. He had a long grayish-white mustache and an even longer goatee. His hands were clasped together, hidden beneath the long-cuffed sleeves of his robe. I watched him intently as he walked slowly down our street towards me. His long robe obscured the movement of his feet giving him the appearance of gliding effortlessly over the pavement. When he finally stopped at arm's length in front of me, I asked who he was. 'Miazon' was the name he gave. I asked if he too, was a prior incarnation of myself, like the others had been. He laughed and said no, that he wasn't. Next I wanted to know about the Cowboy, and the Knight in armor, and the Roman foot soldier. Miazon told me that they were indeed prior incarnations of myself. I also wanted to know where they came from and where he had come from. Although he looked Asian, he didn't look Chinese or Japanese or Korean or for that matter like any other ethnic Asian other than perhaps a little like a Mongolian. Miazon informed me that I myself had inadvertently brought all four of them here. Then, he began to explain how that process unfolded.

I had recently been to 'The Crack in the Earth.' This is a term a Sorcerer would use when referring to that place where the two parallel universes are connected, or are in very close proximity to each other, i.e. 'The Crack in the Earth' which is a narrow canyon with vertical walls of solid rock on either side separated by a deep narrow bottomless crevasse. On each side of the canyon there is a narrow trail cut into the solid rock not more than three feet wide. Whenever I have gone to the 'gateway' to the parallel dimension I have only traveled on the right side of the canyon, when the canyon wall is illuminated by the light from the setting sun. Everyone going there always uses the pathway on the right side of the canyon. The pathway on the left side of the canyon is only for use by travelers coming out of that gateway and into our universe.

I got the bright idea of trying to go into the parallel universe via the pathway on the left side of the canyon. I was the only person going in the wrong direction. Miazon pointed out the fact that while I was heading for the gateway on the left side of the canyon, I brushed against the shoulders of three different men heading in the opposite direction. They were the Cowboy, the Knight, and the Roman foot soldier.

I told Miazon that all of the travelers I had met on the pathway were only wearing loincloths. He laughed and said that all four of them, including he himself, had traveled a long journey through time. He said that he himself had traveled more than three thousand years just to meet me, the one who dared to defy the laws of reality and wander around in the bone-yards of time.

Miazon told me that he is alive and well and lives as we speak in the far distant past. I asked him what ethnicity he was. He told me that this Asian looking character was not really himself but a projection of his own creation that he used when he traveled into our universe. Miazon himself is confined to his own universe, the parallel universe.

Like Miazon I too have developed my own schemes and devices for traveling within his universe, the parallel universe.

Dark Stranger

The night before last the Source took me to a place he referred to as "The River of No Return." He left me standing at its edge without any comment. The river was dark, rusty-brown in color resembling the iron mixture you pour into your swimming pool that ties up organic compounds, so that algae doesn't grow. All of the surroundings were very dark and desolate. The river was flowing slowly from my right side to my left. I assumed he wanted me to somehow cross the river. I could not see how far the other side might actually be. I did eventually cross over after many challenges and ended up in a park with a single ornate cast-iron bench facing in the direction from which I had just come. Out of the darkness a "Dark Stranger" approached. He presented me with a dagger for successfully navigating my way across the river. He said that it was the "Dagger of Death" and it could kill anything or anyone. He left with no further comments. I put the dagger in its sheath and attached it to my belt on the left side for easy access with my right hand.

Last night the Source told me that he was very surprised that I had actually figured out a way to cross the "River of No Return" and survived. He asked if I had met the "Dark Stranger" who inhabits the other side of the "River of No Return." I told him that I had met the Stranger and he had given me a gift. The Source asked to see that gift. When I presented it to the Source, he said that the dagger would not be effective until it had been activated. He brought the dagger to life and its sharpened edges lit up with pulsating luminescent colors. He said that it was now a "Poisoned Dagger" and could indeed kill anything or anyone. I asked the Source who the "Dark Stranger " was and what he did. The Source said that he was like an angel but different. His orientation was actually chaotic-neutral. He was neither evil nor good but like other angels he had great powers and could not be killed.

I asked the Source where angels actually came from. He said that he created angels but once they were created the angels gravitated on their own to whatever orientation and special duties they chose.

Aru

When I returned home from my son's house it was a few minutes before 2:00 a.m. in the morning. There was still time for me to catch the 'Night Bus' which passes by at 2:00 o'clock sharp. I went out in front of the house and waited for the bus to arrive. Not being sure where to go when the bus stopped and the folding door opened, I asked the driver if he could take me to 'Dream Time.' I have been to Dream Time before in the past but the technique that I used, that was shown to me by an Aborigine spirit dancer, was tricky and had a lot of limitations. The Night Bus spiraled downward like a fireman coming down a fire-pole. In no time, the door swung open and I was let out into what looked like a jungle in Hawaii.

A little man approached me with nothing on but a skimpy leather thong. He was no more than four and a half feet tall. His skin was very dark and weathered. His hair was thick, dark and curly. He was definitely Aborigine. The little man introduced himself to me as Aru the keeper of 'Dream Time.' My attire had been transformed into an equally skimpy thong, as I stepped out of the Night Bus. The only other thing I had with me was the containment pouch still attached to the strap of the thong around my waist. Aru pointed at the containment pouch and asked what I had brought to 'Dream Time.' I told him that I didn't know what it was but after telling him the story of how and where I got it, he felt that it was probably someone's recurrent dream or nightmare. If it had been a spirit, it would have been destroyed or displaced by the explosive device that I used. Dreams on the other hand can't be visualized using the tools that I had been using. Those kind of recurrent dreams hang around like a dark cloud that cannot be seen but only sensed in a non-explicit way. They cast a pall over anyone who walks through them.

After hearing that, I was glad I had been able to remove it from my son's driveway. Not knowing what to do with it, I asked Aru if he had any ideas on how I could get rid of it. He told me to open the pouch and let it go. Aru told me that in Dream Time everything exists forever, unlike real time where everything is transitory and exists only for a short period of time. He said that if it didn't belong there in Dream Time it would simply vanish into thin air before our very eyes.

When I opened the bag a shadowy amorphous cloud emerged from within. Then, it disappeared into the dense jungle foliage. I asked what happened to the dream thing. Aru told me that it would continue to exist forever in Dream Time but it would never trouble my son or his family ever again.

When I asked Aru what kind of dream it had been he said the only way to know for sure was for me to track it down and make it pay fifty dollars every day. He laughed and laughed so hard that he almost fell over onto the ground on his head.

I spent a long time there in 'Dream Time' speaking with Aru. He wished me well and said that I was welcome to come again any time to 'Dream Time.'

When I checked the clock again it was 2:17 in the morning.

Tortuga

This morning I was awake at 3:40 a.m. I wondered if anything unusual might be coming down the street in front of my house at 3:45 a.m., so I went out to the sidewalk and waited to see if anything might pass by.

A large annular ring of smoke, or fog, about eighteen inches high and several feet in width rolled by, followed closely by a second annular ring of smoke, and then a third ring, moving down the street like waves on a lake from some large object having been dropped into the water. I had no idea what kind of contraption could possibly create that kind of effect. I waited anxiously, to see what would come.

To my surprise, there was this huge tortoise, which had to weigh three or four hundred pounds. It definitely was not a Galapagos Tortoise. The carapace was different. It looked more like a Giant African Tortoise. It was moving its legs in a very mechanical way to a cadence quite clock-like. Tick-tock, tick-tock, tick-tock, tick-tock. At first I thought it must be a machine, but upon closer investigation, it was surely not. It was definitely alive, stopping for no one.

I approached the tortoise and engaged it in conversation. I asked the tortoise who he was and he told me that he was the Time Tortoise. I asked about the three rings of smoke, or fog, or whatever it was. The tortoise said that the first ring was the future, the second ring was the present, and the third ring, was the past.

As we continued down the road, his pace was unrelenting. I asked why he came at 3:45 in the morning. He said that he came at 3:45 a.m. because he weighed three hundred and forty–five pounds. We were moving rapidly from place to place. I noticed that the tortoise left a trail of sparkly dust, like smoke from an oil-burning car, or a diesel truck going up a steep grade in the mountains. The dust trail strung out behind us as far back into the distance as I could see. I asked the tortoise what that dust trail was. He told me that it was time.

Before long, we were traipsing through Grand Central Station. Surprisingly there weren't that many travelers there. Maybe 3:45 a.m. is not at the height of domestic travel.

A small boy, accompanied by both of his parents, approached me. His hair had fallen out in great patches, and he looked emaciated as though he were dying from cancer, or some other terrible disease. He came up to me and tugged at my pant leg as we passed by. He said, "Please, mister, please give me a little more time."

I asked the Time Tortoise if that trail of sparkling dust could actually give someone more time. The tortoise said that it could. "How much more time," I asked. He said, "Maybe five minutes, maybe five months, maybe five years, it all depends." So, I immediately scooped up a bunch of the dust, and sprinkled it over the little boy's head. His hair returned to normal, and his gaunt features were transformed into that of a normal healthy child. He said, "Thanks, mister. Thanks for giving me more time."

I took out my ever-expansive magic bag that I always carry with me and followed the Time Tortoise, scooping up as much time dust as I could carry because you never know when you might encounter someone who is running out of time and needs just a little more time to finish their job.

Essence of Time

An Allegory:

Last night I engaged the Source in a lengthy discussion. He reminded me, as he often does, that he has no physical form and no gender. The appearance he presents is of my own creation for he is pure energy, pure awareness, pure intent and pure will.

We were standing on the beach looking out onto the calm ocean and the event horizon. He said, "Walk with me," and extended his hand. As we moved from the sand onto the water, the water became solid like ice but not cold and not slippery. Each step we took pushed the solid surface we were walking on further and further out from the sandy beach. When we were far from the shore and the entire surface of the expansive sea was solid, the source told me that it was time for me to understand more about the event horizon and what it really constituted. The ocean we were standing on was really not water and the sandy beach was not sand. The solid surface we were standing on was in reality, time. The sandy beach was the past, the sands of time. All of the events currently transpiring lay under our feet. Future events lay further out ahead of us, there beneath its hard surface.

I bent down and began brushing away a white powdery substance that covered its surface, so that I could see events that were transpiring under our feet.

The white powder was reminiscent to me of the powder that accumulates on surfaces outside, at night, when you live somewhere near an ocean. It seemed to stick to my fingers. I asked the Source what this white stuff was. He told me that it was the 'essence of time.' I am familiar with fairy dust and some of the things that it can do and I am familiar with stardust that is found on the surface of the string formed by our dimension and I'm familiar with some of the things that it can do. The Source told me that the essence of time could do many things and that I should take some with me because it could only be gathered from the solid surface of time, where we were now standing. I scooped up as much as I could and put it into a large leather pouch. I scooped up enough to last me an entire lifetime. When I asked again what it could do, the Source presented his answer to me as an allegory.

"Suppose you were an alien from a place which had no water, and no knowledge of water. How should I explain to you what water was and what it could do when it is everywhere and in everything and is life itself? Such is the essence of time. It is everywhere. It is in everything. Nothing can be done without it. You must discover for yourself how to use it and what you choose to do with it. You have come so very far in your quest for understanding the true nature of reality, but you have a very, very long ways yet to travel. I am curious as to how far you actually make it before your time catches up with you, somewhere in your sleep."

Dust of Time

After going to 'The Place' and recharging as I do daily, the Source asked me to walk with him. His arms were crossed behind his back and his hands were clasped together. As we walked slowly along the hard surface his feet kicked up dust. He said to me, "See this dust, it is the dust of time. It is not only the dust of time but time itself. Time is actually a thing. It actually has physicality. You can actually hold it in your hand. You can store it in a sack. It actually is sand-like. You can walk on it. You can form it into bricks, strange but true. Time does not exist as a solid in your reality or in your world but in other dimensions it does. As a seer, as a wizard, as a time traveler you are ready to make the leap into multiple dimensional realities and multidimensional worlds. That is the challenge that I give you." The Source vanished and I was alone in the vast emptiness.

The River

The other night I was conversing with the Source as we were walking along together when he stopped, looked straight at me and said, "It's time." We proceeded for a ways further until we came to the edge of a river. There wasn't a riverbank and there was no vegetation anywhere. There was just plain brown dirt and plain brown water separated by a knife-edge juncture between the water and the dirt.

He said to me, "This is the river." I could barely detect a very slow movement of the water in the river, but just barely. The surface of the water was flat and smooth and the river was very wide. I couldn't make out the other side clearly. It was too far away.

The Source said, " This is the river of time. To the left is the future. To the right is the past. Directly in front of us is the present. If you walk on the ground on the edge of the river in either direction, when you turn to face the river it will always be the present. If you walk on the surface of the river itself to your right you will move into the past. If you walk to your left on the surface of the river it will always be the present because no mater at what pace you proceed up river, the flow of the river of time will always match the speed at which you walk up stream, keeping you always in the present moment.

If you go over to the other side of the river, facing us, you can walk into the future or into the past by walking on the ground next to the river. If you walk to your left you will move into the future and if you walk to your right you will walk into the past. The further you walk on the edge of the river, the further you move forward or backwards in time, when you turn and face the river.

The challenge is in getting over to the other side of the river of time. You cannot walk across on the surface of the river and you cannot go by portal because on this side of the river time moves in one direction and on the other side of the river times moves in the opposite direction. The only way for you to get to the other side is to use the Black Door to Anywhere." He vanished leaving me standing at the edge of the 'River of Time.'

Take It to the Limit

Last night while I was walking with the Source he looked up at the sky and asked me what I saw up there. I didn't see anything, absolutely nothing. Then he looked down at the surface we were walking on and asked me what I saw down there. I didn't see anything, absolutely nothing. He asked me to look to my left and to my right and wanted to know what I saw there. My answers were the same, absolutely nothing. Then, he turned to me and said, "Take it to the limit. Give it your best effort."

I was completely baffled by his request. The first thing I did was to go to 'the place' to store up as much energy as I could because I had no idea what might transpire from this request.

I thought about catching the night plane that comes at 1:00 o'clock but decided that might not be such a great idea. The same thing happened when the night bus came by at 2:00 o'clock in the morning. It just didn't feel right. It didn't feel like that was what I should do.

Before the night train came by at 4:00 o'clock I got a few things together and went out to wait for the train to come by. When the conductor got down from the train and asked me where I wanted to go I told him I wanted to "Take It to the Limit." He told me to tell the engineer up in the cab and yelled as loud as he could, "All aboard." I was the only one standing there.

When I told the engineer what I wanted to do, he got up from his seat and turned the controls of the old steam engine over to me. I had no idea what I was doing and no idea what I should be doing. I know steam engines can actually run pretty fast depending on how much pressure you can get up in an old boiler like this engine had.

"Take it to the limit," what did that mean? I put the engine in reverse and backed it up slowly until the slack was taken out of the couples. They use to do that when I was a kid watching the steam engines come and go on the Southern Pacific Railroad. Then, I eased it forward so we didn't spin the drive wheels as the train started to move. It began slowly increasing speed. I checked the pressure gauge as the needle creped past 100 PSI. I thought I might end up blowing the boiler apart trying to take it to the limit. Then I asked myself the question, taking what to the limit? For me that was the real issue. Taking what to the limit? No one said I had to take this train to its maximum speed. That would surely end badly with a driver who didn't even know how to stop this thing. Instead I decided to take it to the limit in terms of maximum distance traveled with the existing load of coal in the coal-car.

I got it up to twenty-eight miles per hour and kept it there with the boiler pressure on the low end of the green scale on the pressure gauge. We ended up stopping for water several times but in the end we finally ran out of steam when the coal ran out. We had made it all the way to the town of Show Low in the White Mountains. That was a real accomplishment, in and of itself.

When I saw the Source he told me that he was very surprised. He thought I would go for the maximum speed and the maximum boiler pressure and probably blow the boiler apart. He was surprised that instead I went for the distance. I took the distance to the limit instead. I had given it my best effort. I had been shrewd.

The Gift

About two weeks ago, while conversing with the Source, something that all sorcerers aspire to do, he asked me to put out my hand because he had a gift for me. Being right-handed, I reached out with my right hand. He said no, the other hand, so I obliged. No sorcerer in their right mind would even think of not accepting a gift, any gift from the Source, when they had expended untold years and unimaginable effort just to locate the Source, not to mention being able to establish a personal conversational relationship with the Source.

The Source placed an object about the size of a large chicken egg in my palm. It had a flat base, so it stood upright in my hand with sort of a rounded point at the top, like a small artichoke but more slender like the tip of an asparagus. It resembled a large flower bud from some kind of a plant but it seemed to be made of some kind of metal. I stared down at it for a while and eventually asked what it was.

The Source said it was the gift of understanding. It had nothing to do with intellect, or with knowledge, just as knowledge has nothing to do with wisdom. "You come from a knowledge-based world where there is little wisdom and almost no understanding. You are ready for the gift of understanding. This gift will serve you well."

I stared at the object in my hand and as I did so, it began slowly opening. As I watched, it turned into a large beautiful flower. Then, it began to radiate some kind of pulsating light. The flower sank slowly into my open palm and disappeared.

With that, the Source vanished and I was left standing alone, staring down at my empty, open hand.

Three Crows

Every month, on the full moon, a gift or gifts arrive, delivered by magic crows. This month I checked for the crows at the height of the full moon, but no crows were to be found anywhere. We were away from home, high up in the mountains at the cabin for the weekend. So, I transported down to our home in the city far below on the desert floor. There in the living room were three, very, very large crows rough housing and carrying on like juvenile delinquents. I told them to follow me up to the cabin in the pines. They followed sheepishly, having been caught off their guard misbehaving.

These three crows were each more than three feet tall. They began goofing around like the Three Stooges, there next to my bed. I said, "Look guys, what gifts do you have to deliver?" They just kept acting silly and goofing around.

Finally one of the crows sauntered up to the bed and spat out several kernels of corn or some kind of seeds. The second crow and then the third crow did the same thing. They cackled loudly at each other, and then they stared at me for a moment before flying off into the moonlit night sky. Seeds were scattered all over the place. They were on the bed, on the floor, and some were even underneath the bed. I thought that they were really nuts of some kind but they turned out to actually be some kind of strange seeds. I had no idea what this whole event was all about, so I enlisted the help of the Facilitator. He told me that the seeds were magical and were supposed to be planted in the light of the full moon.

I said, "This is the night of the full moon. I'll plant them right now, why wait?" So, I gathered up as many of the seeds as I could find and planted them all around me in a circular pattern, then I went to sleep. When I awoke, the next morning, there were vines about four feet tall growing in a circle all around me. I thought of Jack and the Bean Stalk. But as the vines grew taller and taller, they increasingly began to slope outwards.

Finally, they all lay down prostrate on the surface of the ground each heading off in a different direction. It was hard to count their exact number accurately because of their rapid growth but there were approximately twenty of these vines. As the vines continued their rapid growth, they coalesced into a solid circle around me and then separated into twenty separate pathways, each wide enough to walk upon.

No one knows where these pathways may lead, but I will surely have to investigate each and every one of them. But first, I need to pack a large lunch. You never know how long you will be gone when you follow twenty different paths to their very end.

Twinkle, Twinkle, Willow Tree

I never re-visited the magical plants with their prostrate coalesced stalks which formed pathways leading outward in every direction from their central circle as they emerged from the ground and had sprouted from the magical seeds delivered by the three crows that arrived with the last full moon. I was looking for something to do instead of counting sheep that I'm not that good at. So, I returned to where these magical plants spread out from their point of origin. It was reminiscent of the roundabouts in Ireland. I began walking counter clockwise around and around this roundabout.

The first time around, I saw nothing. The second time around I saw a small house in one direction and what looked like an aerial fireworks display far, far away. The third time around I saw a second house off in another direction and that same fireworks display closer and brighter. That obviously was where I needed to go. Who can ignore an aerial fireworks display? Certainly not me.

The closer I got to the second house, the bigger and brighter the display became. At some point, it became obvious to me that the twinkling was not coming from fireworks, but from a tree, a willow tree whose leaves were all different colors, shiny, bright, and fluttering on its many drooping branches. I thought this was so cool. I had to go and sit down under all of those glittering leaves. I asked, "What kind of tree is this?" The answer came from the tree itself. "The Tree of Wisdom!"

As soon as I sat down under this huge willow tree and rested my back against its broad trunk, the tree started to shrink. The branches seemed to have very little substance as they shrank in around me. The shrinking continued until the tree was only a foot tall. I picked it up and placed it on my right shoulder. This is great, I thought, wisdom on my right shoulder. The tree then hopped up on top of my head and the trunk sank down until it disappeared, leaving only its tiny branches hanging down all around my head.

In front of me, a landscape materialized. There was a green, green, pasture with Golden Guernsey cows grazing. Off to the right side of the pasture was a huge pear tree. It was magnificent. It was the most beautiful pear tree I have ever seen. I think a pear tree is the most beautiful tree there is, with its broad crown, standing alone on the crest of a hill. I immediately walked over and sat down under its dense shade, admiring this perfect pastoral scene.

As soon as I leaned back against its trunk, spring water began bubbling out of the ground, flowing down the hill. The spring flowed into a stream. The stream flowed into a river, and the river flowed into a lake. In the middle of the lake, a small round island emerged. In its center was a single round stone about four-feet in diameter. I went out to the island, sat down on the rock, and looked back across the lake to where I could see myself sitting under the pear tree. At the same time, I looked out from under the pear tree and could see myself sitting on top of the rock in the middle of the island, in the middle of the lake.

Then I knew that I was observing the path of wisdom. To be able to see and to understand what was at the end of a journey, as well as to see what was at the beginning of the journey, even before you take that first step, "That is the Essence of Wisdom."

A Bridge too Far

I went to the beach to meet up with the Facilitator. He was sitting on that same park bench with the child. I sat down between them. The Facilitator said that it was time for me to go into the fog bank by myself but I was not to step in the water. I was supposed to clear the fog and calm the surface of the water. I walked slowly into the fog alone, took out my rose-colored glasses and made my way up to the edge of the water but I did not get my feet wet. I tried everything I could think of but nothing seemed to get rid of the fog or to calm the turbulent waters. After about forty minutes, I returned to the bench where the Facilitator and the child were sitting. I said that I was tired and I needed to take a break but that I would return later to try again. Then I left.

An hour or so later, I went back to try again. This time I took the child with me and I summoned the Other and together we made our way through the fog to the edge of the water. We moved our arms in unison and the fog cleared, then, we calmed the waters with our synchronous movements. In the distance, at the edge of the event horizon there was what appeared to be a bunch of white birds flying around in a chaotic circular pattern. I put on the rose-colored glasses and the birds became white spots and in their midst appeared a skeleton that was walking step by step closer and closer. Then I pulled out the sword of truth and looked at the reflection of the skeleton in its shimmering surface. The white spots became black dots swarming around like a hive of bees. The skeleton came closer and I could see a hole in its forehead that was in the shape of a cross. I knew then, that what was approaching was my death.

I instinctively reached out and grabbed the child's hand on my right side. The skeleton stopped dead in its tracks. I reached out with my left hand and grasped the hand of the Other, on my left side. The skeleton and the black dots fizzled and disappeared back into the water.

We turned around together and went back to the park bench on the beach. The Facilitator in the gray suit was standing there, as we approached. He said that he was no longer needed here, that I had learned how to function within the event horizon, that the skeleton was my death, and that I had successfully elicited the butterfly effect and thereby had once again cheated my own death. He turned and walked away into the night, leaving the three of us there alone.

I walked away in the opposite direction, crossed a bridge and looked back, knowing that you could not share my crossing, for this bridge and what I encountered on the other side of this bridge, was indeed a bridge too far and there was no way that you could possibly follow where I had gone or comprehend what I had experienced.

Adept's School of Knowledge

I awoke early Saturday morning and found myself wearing a black cotton robe with its hood hanging down on my back and long black pajama-like pants. My head was shaved, and I was wearing sandals. I looked up and saw a lot of adult males similarly dressed all coming from different directions headed towards this large square brick building five stories high in front of us. On the face of the building up near its top, in large letters, was the name, "Adept School of Knowledge."

Last night, I was working in the third attention, the place of emptiness, when the Source suggested that I revisit the Adept School of Knowledge, so I opened a portal and transported over there. No one was around.

I entered through the double doors. The door on the right side opened inward, and the door on the left side opened outward. Inside there was a long hallway about two meters wide, and more than a hundred meters in length. There were no doorways, nor were there any light fixtures or switches anywhere, yet there was an even level of illumination. The walls, the floor and the ceiling were all a uniform light-gray color. I walked the entire length of the hall. It ended in a 'T' shaped intersection with an identical hallway at right angles going to the left, and to the right. I turned left and went down that hallway. It was the same as the one I had just traversed, with no doors, light fixtures or switches, and a uniform level of illumination. I followed it to its end where it turned ninety degrees to the left. At the end of each hall there was another left turn. This continued as each hall became shorter, like a maze in a cornfield, until it finally ended in a square room a little more than two meters in dimension. The entrance disappeared creating a square space.

In the center of the room was a square pillow on the floor, with a Chinese-style lady's folding hand fan on top of it. It was a pillow like the ones people use to sit on when they meditate. Instead of picking up the fan and sitting down on the pillow, I took out my rose-colored glasses which allows me to see things as they are instead of how they appear to be, and the fan now appeared to be a tall white wading bird, like a crane. The pillow became a big pile of bird droppings.

Next I took out the double-lensed, magical pince-nez spectacles that show things as they really are, and the bird droppings turned into a pile of gold coins, while the white bird became a creature comprised of pure energy. Then, I took out the 'sword of truth' whose reflection shows the true nature of something, and the pile of gold coins were replaced with a bottomless black hole, and the creature made of energy turned into a wisp of spiraling smoke. I swung the sword with great force striking the cloud of smoke. Everything instantly disappeared. I was alone in the room with the pillow and the fan. The room was oriented with each corner pointing in a cardinal direction. I re-oriented the pillow and sat down facing west. I positioned the fan pointing north, meditated, and entered the place of emptiness where only the Source exists. I heard a humming sound…mmm, that grew and became a defining AHHH… It was the sound of a thousand meditating monks chanting their mantras. I became the sound itself.

The Source said to me, "I see that you have just had your first lesson at the Adept School of Knowledge." I asked the Source, "What was the lesson and what was I supposed to have learned from that whole experience." The source said to me, "The first and most important lesson is, 'Nothing is what it appears to be'…ever!"

Absolute

Last night, before I went to sleep, I was talking with the Source. He said, "Walk with me." As we walked along side by side he instantly shrank to the size of a small mouse. I thought this was really weird. After a few more steps he became a huge giant many stories tall, before he finally returned to his normal size, which in itself is quite impressive. I was really quite surprised by the whole experience and so I asked him what that was all about. He of course asked me what was what all about. When I shared my experience, with him being tiny one minute then gigantic the next he replied, " I am the source of all things. I am the alpha and the omega. I am unchanging. I am the absolute. I have not changed in the slightest. It is you who first became gigantic thinking I had shrunk to the size of a mouse. Then you became extremely small and thought that I had become a giant. It is not I that changed size but you who have changed your size. You must contemplate upon that which has just transpired." With that he disappeared and left me standing alone in the darkness to sort out what had just occurred. I went to sleep while thinking about this recent encounter with the Source.

A Different Path to Follow

A few nights ago, the Source took me to a pathway and said that this was the path I should follow. The Source had never done anything like that before. Everything was always left up to me to make all of the decisions and do all of the choosing. If the Source were willing to point out a path, I certainly would follow it. We walked together down the winding path for quite a ways. There was absolutely nothing on either side of the pathway. In the distance stood a solitary tree. We continued down the path until we finally arrived under this very large tree. I asked what kind of tree it was. The Source told me that it was the Tree of Treasures and that I should stay there under it until I had acquired all of the riches that I desired. I stayed there one night. The tree was filled with all kinds of gold and jewels and other things of great value.

While traveling from one destination to another, I passed an Asian man with short dark hair, who was wearing a scarlet robe, standing on the side of the road facing oncoming traffic. I zoomed past in my haste but later decided to return in search of this scarlet-robed man, who seemed so out of place. When I finally found him, I asked him if he were a monk or a Buddhist Priest or perhaps a Buddha. He said yes. I'm not sure what that answer meant but I left it at that.

I asked the sojourner in the red robe if he would like to walk with me for a ways and he agreed to join me. We walked down the new pathway to where the Tree of Treasures was. I told him about the tree and then I asked if he would continue down the path a bit farther to see where it might lead. He asked if I had gotten all of the riches I desired. I told him that it wasn't human nature to ever get all of the riches one might desire but that I needed to continue along the pathway. I couldn't stay longer under the Tree of Treasures. So, we followed the winding pathway until we came to another tree.

From it hung hundreds of framed pictures, each with the portrait of someone from my life. This was the Tree of Family and Friends. We continued on together down the path. I put on the rose-colored glasses, and the man in the scarlet robe became a skeleton walking beside me in the red robe. I returned the glasses to the pocket where they were usually stored, before continuing the conversation with this man of religion. Eventually we came to a huge eucalyptus tree with a single Koala bear in its branches. I climbed up into the tree and addressed the Koala bear. When I asked about the eucalyptus tree, and what he was doing there, the Koala bear said that he was born in that tree and spent his entire life in that tree, as had his entire family. I put the rose-colored glasses on and found myself looking at the skeleton of a dead Koala bear up in the burned out skeleton of a dead eucalyptus tree in the midst of a burned and dead eucalyptus forest somewhere in the outback of Australia.

I climbed down out of the eucalyptus tree and

continued along the path alone until I came to a small cul-de-sac. The path had obviously come to its end. As I turned and looked back along the path I had taken, I saw myself sitting under the Tree of Treasures and under the Tree of Family and Friends and up in the eucalyptus tree talking with the live Koala bear and also in the burned-out eucalyptus tree with the skeleton of the dead Koala bear. Then I understood why the Source wanted me to take that path. It was a lesson in impermanence, a lesson in the transient nature of life and the circular path that it follows.

The man in the scarlet robe and I returned to the beginning of the path. Then we went over and sat down on the park bench, on the beach, in front of the ocean with the event horizon in the distance. The Facilitator joined us. The three of us sat there together in silence, looking out on the sea and the event horizon.

A raft appeared in the distance and came slowly towards us until it finally came to rest in the sand at the edge of the water. I was sitting on the raft and I was the oarsman standing behind myself and I was sitting on the bench between the man in the red robe and the Facilitator and I was also sitting under the Tree of Treasures and under the Tree of Family and Friends and I was up in the eucalyptus tree with the Koala bear.

I stood and walked slowly to the edge of the water, bent down and scooped up a glass of water and offered it to myself on the raft, and then to myself as the oarsman and finally I too drank a toast to life, me myself and I. They turned and rowed off into the horizon, my death and I together on the raft of life and I returned to my place sitting on the park bench between the Facilitator and the holy man in the scarlet robe.

Last night, I returned to the third attention to give myself a break. I asked the Source there about the process of having gone down that path. He clarified a few of the elements in that project. The two eucalyptus trees that had the two different Koala bears in them, was in reality only one tree, The Tree of Life and Death. The cul-de-sac was a different place in reality from which to perceive events. The man in the scarlet robe was The Traveler's Buddha, who can only be encountered when one is actively traveling through reality from one point of observation to another point of observation of reality itself.

The Plunge

Late this morning at around 5:30 a.m., I was talking with the Source as we walked in the place of complete emptiness. He furrowed his brow, squinted looking over towards me and said, "I think you are ready to take the plunge." I had no idea what he was referring to.

He asked me to look all around and tell him what I saw. I saw nothing in front of us, nothing behind us, nothing to our right, nothing to our left, nothing above us and nothing below us. There was nothing anywhere.

He stopped and a verdant green valley appeared in front of us. It was bowl-shaped surrounded by high mountains with a small stream traversing it from the right to the left. The whole scene was round and beautiful but surrounded by nothingness. As we stood on a ridge looking down at this idyllic scene he said that it was time for me to choose. Of course I wanted to know what he was talking about. My concept of 'taking the plunge' obviously needed some clarification.

"You have demonstrated the stupidity of a moron and the caution of an idiot. That scene before you is the world of the messenger. Once you enter into it you may never escape from it. It is your choice, to take that plunge or to not take that plunge. The task of a messenger is to deliver the message, no other. It is true you have been given the gift of a great seer and the gift of a great healer and the gift of time travel. These are all essential tools necessary to acquire a message but they are not in and of themselves the message."

True to form, I of course asked, "How do I enter?" He said to me, "Open your chest as though you were removing a sports coat" and I did. I found myself in the middle of this huge valley ringed by high mountains standing next to the burbling stream.

Ark

Late this morning, around 4:30 a.m., I was talking with the Source. He told me that he wanted to talk with me about the concept of ark. I of course mentioned Noah and his ark and the Ark of the Covenant since those are arks that I am familiar with. He began his explanation with the two of them and then, moved on to expand his conversation to describe what an 'ark' is. He explained to me that an ark is essentially a safe place to store something of value.

So Noah's Ark was a place of safety from the flood for Noah, his family and many animals important to his locality and livelihood. The Ark of the Covenant was a place of safety to store and transport what was basically a contract between God and a nomadic tribe of people, the House of Israel.

The Source wanted me to become the ark of consciousness. He gave me the gift of awareness to share with others. He expanded upon this and said as a seer can see or a healer can heal, so to a dispenser of consciousness can make the blind man see or the deaf man hear for when you are awake your awareness sleeps and though your eyes are open you are blind and though you hear, your awareness is deaf and though you speak you say nothing.

So the ark of consciousness is the place where awareness is safely stored. The Source once again reminded me that the children I treat daily are the ones who have taught me how to shift my awareness and how to move consciousness from one place to another. They would help me to master this, the gift of consciousness, which was freely given and should therefore be freely shared.

A Time to Choose

Last night the Source asked me to walk with him. It was apparent that he was uncertain as how best to present the next challenge he had in store for me. He furrowed his brow and asked me to tell him what I saw to my left, to my right and straight-ahead in front. I looked all around and saw nothing, only blackness in every direction. He frowned and said, "You must choose a direction in which to travel. You may turn left or right or go straight ahead. There is no turning back." I saw only blackness in every direction.

The Source added, "If you go forward straight ahead, death awaits you. If you turn to the right, death is waiting for you. If you turn to the left, you will surely die." That all sounded really great. But, I still needed to choose from one of the three directions.

Since it always appears easier to continue going straight ahead in the direction that you are currently moving rather than turning abruptly to the left or to the right, I tried to discern what lay directly in front of me first. I projected my awareness out into the darkness as far as possible. This is what I saw: There was a thin young blond woman standing alone facing me. When I observed her through the rose-colored glasses she appeared to be poorly dressed and dirty with disheveled hair. When I used the double-lensed pince-nez spectacles she appeared emaciated wearing tattered rags. With the reflection from the sword of truth she was a skeleton. When I used the wizard's powers of perception she became a miniature 'Grim Reaper.'

Next I turned and faced to the right projecting my awareness as far as possible out into the darkness. What I saw was an African American female standing alone facing me. With the rose-colored glasses she appeared to be poorly dressed with ratty hair. With the double-lensed pince-nez spectacles, she too became emaciated and dressed in rags. And, with the reflection from the sword of truth she became a skeleton. With the powers of observation of a wizard she too became a 'Grim Reaper.'

Then, I turned around and faced the other direction. There I saw a large rectangular window encased in its wooden frame. When I observed the framed window through the rose-colored glasses, it was transformed into a large sliding patio glass door. With the double-lensed pince-nez spectacles, the door was open and with the reflection from the sword of truth, the figure of the 'Thinker' appeared seated on his rock in silhouette facing straight ahead instead of looking at me. With the power of the wizard's perception I became the 'Thinker' and an open door into the 'corridor' appeared.

Since I have previously entered the first two doors on the right side of the corridor and the first two doors on the left side, I chose to enter the third doorway on the right side of the corridor. As I entered it became the beautiful 'secret garden' I have visited many times before first as a small child then later as a middle school child and now again as a young man. This same young blond lady met me and extended her hand to me. We held hands and walked together into the lush green garden as it engulfed us. I asked what her name was and she replied, "Robin." I knew then that this was the direction I would choose. I told the Source that I had chosen to turn left. He vanished leaving me alone to ponder upon my future.

Global Perspective

Last night I was talking with the Source. He told me that it was time for me to be able to observe the world from a hemispherical perspective, like in a planetarium or using a fish-eye lens. He wanted me to acquire the ability to observe the world from every direction simultaneously. He said that to actually accomplish that feat I would have to engage all twelve eyes at the same time. Then he explained what he was referring to when he said all twelve eyes. That would be two normal eyes from each of the four cardinal directions plus the third eye from each direction totaling twelve. Sort of like a compound eye from an insect. I really had no idea how I might possibly be able to accomplish that trick.

Later when the night plane was coming by at 1:00 o'clock I ventured out to the street in front of our house to await its arrival. I waited for the sound of an airplane to approach but there was nothing, no sound, no plane, no nothing. I was ready to go back inside when an apparatus attached to a single cord was lowered onto my head. It was reminiscent of a helmet that I once encountered in a very advanced aircraft some time ago. When it was secured in place I could see in any direction 360 degrees. This was what I needed to accomplish in a global way. I decided to go to Wizard Island and attempt to accomplish this feat there inside the cave where I would be isolated and protected from harm. I sat down in the middle of the cavernous space and began to meditate.

Out of the sky above me dropped this dome like bowl suspended by a single wire. I put it on my head and was then able to see in all four cardinal directions simultaneously. It helped me to make the transition from seeing in only one or two directions to being able to see in all four directions at the same time.

It took some effort but eventually I was successful and managed to see in a global way in every direction simultaneously with what appeared to me to be a seamless integration of all the different fields of vision.

When I discussed this personal advancement with the Source he told me that there were actually twenty-seven separate perspectives in the global view of reality. That's a lot of slices to splice together at the same time. I obviously need to do a lot more work on this process.

Gazing

The next night after accomplishing the task of seeing from a hemispherical perspective, the Source said it was time for me to re-visit the art of 'gazing.' Gazing is a process of using your eyes to gather information about something that is much more intrusive and inclusive than what you can gather by looking at the external appearance of something. It is an important tool used by sorcerers to accomplish many different things.

I was instructed to practice gazing on Wizard Island inside the conical hollow Wizard Mountain where it would be safe from all of the many things transpiring outside this cavernous space. I had been here a few years ago but I had no idea what it was or that it was located on Wizard Island. I didn't even know that such a place even existed. At that time I referred to this place in 'King on the Mountain.' I will repeat that experience for you here as either a reminder if you have read it in the past or as a reference to the spiral process by which I eventually gain a broader perspective of something when I eventually re-visit it.

My first efforts at gazing were with small inanimate objects. I worked my way around my environment there inside the cavern, before I worked my way outside of the safety of the hollow mountain. I sat and gazed out through the large opening where the dragons had entered the mountain on the lee side of the mountain. From that vantage point I could see the myriad threads streaming past that were sustaining physical reality. I also learned through gazing that the threads were not continuous but in fact coded information either attached to these threads or streaming down them incrementally at a very rapid rate. I was observing the future becoming the past.

While investigating the interior of this realm within the mountain, I came upon the sword and armor that I had donned when I was here years ago. I learned through gazing that these items belonged to the King of Titans. From that I surmised that this must have been where Titans once lived. That means that Titans must have been more than mythical creatures but powerful users of magic. There were none here now so something must have happened to them sometime in the past.

Over time I worked my way out of the mountain and up its steep sides, all the way up to its top. By becoming a pinpoint awareness and engaging the

360-degree global perspective I was able to see into the oncoming threads of reality. By moving outside of time instantaneously I observed not only the source of reality streaming straight up out of its origin but also how and where it was bent ninety degrees by time. Beyond this eruption of reality lay the engine of creation spewing something into this sea of threads and bending them ninety degrees and imbuing them with time.

After sharing my experience with the Source he told me that I had witnessed the dreams emerging from the Dreamer, the source of all physical reality and I had located the engine of creation. It was now time for me to try my hand at creation. Since I was now the only living wizard, the Sapphire Wizard, I needed to create a pattern, a mold and energize it with emotion. I told the Source that I had no idea how to create a mold or even what a mold was made of but the answers must be here somewhere on Wizard's Island.

Princess of the Pale

Early this morning sometime after midnight the Source said to me, "Michael, walk with me." As we walked he held his hands clasped behind his back looking down as though in deep thought. I followed his lead and put my hands behind my back and looked down glancing occasionally at him from the side. After a few moments he said, "It is time for you to see the pale." I responded, "Like beyond the pale?"

In front of us appeared this shear fabric curtain, which was obviously the "Pale." He stood in front of the pale for a moment then in what looked to me like a quick karate move he whirled on his left heel and ripped open a big hole in the pale with his right hand that appeared to me to have been a large claw of some kind that was over two feet in length. We walked through the hole in the pale and he asked me to tell him what I saw.

I saw only blackness and nothing else. He said that this was the realm of the dead and it was separated from the world of the living by the pale. At that moment a young blond women who resembled 'Lady Gaga' flew by. She was wearing a shimmering transparent costume. She spun around in front of me and then she was gone. I asked the Source if she were Lady Gaga. The Source said, as he stooped down and picked up the sheer garment that she was wearing from the floor, "She was the Princess of the Pale." She had left that piece of the pale he had torn from the fabric of the curtain, which separated the living from the dead. He said that I was to close the opening he had made in the pale with that missing piece of fabric. Otherwise, the dead could come into the world of the living not as ghosts but as living dead. I said, "Like the Zombie apocalypse?" His response was, "No, not zombies... living dead. You may enter the world of the dead through this opening but you must always replace the torn fabric to keep the dead from returning to the world of the living."

When I got up this morning to go to the bathroom I stepped on a pile of sheer fabric that came from the pale. I had forgotten to cover the opening last night when we left the world of the dead. I hastily returned to that spot and replaced the missing fabric, hoping that not too many of the living dead had made their way back into our world, the world of the living.

Flanders Fields

I was walking with the Source last night. He asked me if I knew where we were. I told him that I had no idea where we were. He said, "In Flanders Fields." As we walked along wisps of smoke puffed out of the ground and shot up into the night sky. He asked if I knew what all those wisps of smoke were. Again I told him that I had no idea. The Source said they were the spirits of soldiers who died in World War I. He said that he had been here many times encouraging these many departed young soldiers to come out from hiding in their respective shallow graves but none would ever do so because they felt guilty and were too afraid of what the Source might do to them, to leave the safety of their respective graves but when I accompanied the

Source, they quickly came forth and departed for their unknown futures because they felt safe in my presence. I have no idea why that would be the case. After the Source departed, leaving me alone in Flanders Fields, I continued to walk the entire area where all of these spirits have remained for the past hundred years. With my passing they continued to pour forth from beneath the green grasses, where poppies once grew, in Flanders Fields.

I chanced upon the grave of one, Tyler Moore, dead by age seventeen. That seemed very young to me to come to the end of one's life so violently. I was drawn to this particular grave by a sense of great sadness and futility. As I contemplated Tyler's passing at such a young age I sensed movement out of the corner of one eye. I asked perchance could that be the ghost of Tyler Moore. The answer came back as a yes. He lied to get into the army and died not as the hero he envisioned but as a gut shot kid sorrowful and fearful of death's coming. He never forgave himself for the untold sadness his pointless demise inflicted upon his mother and his friends. I assured him that they were all now, long since dead and buried and surely awaiting his arrival where they would rejoice at his homecoming. Excited he departed, last of all in leaving Flanders Fields, where poppies once grew.

Comfort Zone

Last night I was walking with the Source. Of late he has clasped his arms behind his back apparently in deep thought as he is looking down at the area in front of where we are walking. He stopped and hesitated for a moment before he asked, "Michael, tell me what you see?"

I looked all around and told the Source that I didn't see anything. Then he wanted to know what I could hear. I of course didn't hear a thing but to be completely honest I told him the only thing I heard was a low background noise that I have been aware of for many years, what is often referred to as tinnitus. That just seems to come with age but I didn't think that was what he was asking me about.

He said that as one ages, the clarity of information perceived by your sensory organs deteriorates. That is just a reality of the human condition. He elaborated further, "When you are here in this place and see nothing, hear nothing, sense nothing, you are within your own comfort zone. That should be a sign for you to move along and challenge yourself. You can use that as an indicator that you are not learning, not acquiring new skills, not gaining ground and not making any progress. When you begin to see things, to hear things, to feel things in this place that is a sign that you are back on track. You must force yourself to press on. Time is not your ally. Time is not your friend. Time is the measure and the beat of all things. The challenge for you is to become master of 'Time' itself.

The object is not to be comfortable but to be uncomfortable, very uncomfortable. That is the only way you learn."

Nine Faces

I was busy last night doing onsite research for the next book, Star Quest: Navigator. I was tired and felt I should go to 'The Place' and recharge. I situated myself there in the silence and emptiness when all of a sudden, one face after another popped up in front of me. There were a total of nine different faces. Some were African. Some were from Mexico or South America. Some were from the sub-continent. One was Aborigine. One was a boy about nine years of age. All were of brown skin color. None were white and none were black, only different shades of brown. They were all males. One had ornamental scars all around his face. At that point, the Source appeared.

I asked him who all the faces were. He asked me who I thought they were. I told him that I thought they were all prophets or seers. A door appeared out of nothingness. The Source said the answer lay behind that door. I got up from where I was sitting, walked over to the door and opened it.

On the other side of the door was a cave that sloped downward. I entered the cave and the door vanished leaving me standing in the middle of the sloping cave. I walked down the cave until it ended in a pool of water. The cave was obviously flooded. I stared into the surface of the water and I could see movement beneath its surface. I put my face into the water and I was completely under the water staring up at its surface. I was in a medical office of some kind but it wasn't my office. A young blond teen-age girl came up to me and said," Now you have found the gateway to Prophecy."

Everything vanished in an instant and I was lying on my back in bed staring up at the dark ceiling above.

Prophecy

Last night I worked on several projects before going to 'The Place' to recharge. While I was there I decided to check out the door that led to the tunnel. At first the tunnel appeared to be the same but when I arrived at the area that was flooded, the water was all gone. Perhaps something I did drained it away. Instead of water there was an enlarged opening in the tunnel that was about fifteen feet in diameter. That's how the tunnel ended. I sat down in the middle of the enlarged area. The nine faces from the night before complete with their bodies appeared. The young nine-year old boy stood right in front of me.

I asked him if he were a seer or a prophet. He asked me, "What's the difference."

I said to him that I wasn't sure if there was a difference.

He said, "A seer sees ... a prophet tells others what he has seen." Then, he disappeared. Each of the other eight seers and prophets disappeared after they shared their own perspectives regarding prophecy. The one next to the boy on his right side, my left side, was an Aborigine with teardrop ornamental scars across his forehead and down onto his face. When I turned my attention to him he said, "A seer sees with his eyes. A prophet speaks with his mouth." Then, he too disappeared.

Standing next to the boy on his left side, which was my right, there was a Tibetan monk. He proclaimed, "My eyes know many things. My lips speak only kindness." With these words, he too disappeared. Next to him, to his left, was a Native American medicine man. I immediately recognized him. He said to me, "We are all of many minds but of one spirit." Then he vanished.

Next to the Aborigine on his right side stood a tall witch doctor. He appeared to be from the Caribbean. He had lots of strange tattoos and ornamental scars everywhere. He held a small object tightly in his left hand. It appeared to be a voodoo doll. He said, "A seer breathes air. A prophet breathes only fire." Then, he was gone.

Next to him was an African witch doctor. He said, "See with your eyes. Speak with your lips but touch only with your heart." Then he vanished.

Next to the Native American medicine man was an Indian from South America. He could have been an Inca but I couldn't say for sure. He said to me, " Your feet know the path they should follow. Your tongue knows the story it should tell but your mind moves too much." With that he also vanished. Next to him stood an Arab, one with a thin sharp nose dressed as a Persian. He said only, "The answer lies in your mind."

The last one who was standing behind me, directly opposite the young boy, looked like he was from India. He was barefoot and without a shirt. His long matted hair and beard contrasted with his tattered loincloth. He reached out and touched my forehead saying, "I give you now, the gift of prophecy" then he too vanished.

Down & Down We Go

Last night the Source asked me to walk with him. We walked out on the surface of the ocean. When we were far from land we started to go down like we were in an elevator, in a large glass tube. We kept going down deeper and deeper into the ocean. When we reached the bottom we just kept going down in this clear glass tube. We went down through sedimentary layers, igneous layers and eventually into the molten metal core of the earth. While we were standing in the midst of all this glowing liquid metal the source expounded, "As you have just observed for yourself, there was no Hell, no Hades and no Underworld that we passed through."

Hell is a place but it is not a physical place and it isn't located beneath our feet under the ground. Likewise Hades is a place but not a physical place. It isn't under the ground either but it is very dark and populated with Demons while Hell is populated with Devils. The Underworld is also a place but it too is not a physical place like our world but it is a world none-the-less just as Purgatory and Heaven are also places. When we preface these places with the directional term "down" it doesn't mean that they are actually located 'down' under the ground but that they are below where we are in status and below where we aspire to go.

I have been to all of these referenced places. They really do exist just as Devils, Demons and Monsters of all sorts exist.

Eye of the Storm

Early this morning I was talking with the Source. He said that he wanted to show me something. We took one step and we were standing in the prow of a fishing boat. It was almost twenty feet long, all made of wood and completely open like a skiff. Towards the back of the boat there were several fishermen who were roughly clad in homespun clothing, which was in a bad state of repair. There was a single wood mast where a sail should have been but it had been blown away by the terrible storm we were in. Huge waves and rain driven by gale force winds lashed at the feeble boat. Ominous thunderclouds tumbled down upon us. Disaster was imminent.

The Source stretched out his arm and the sea became smooth and the wind was calmed. Sunlight broke through the clouds and the sky became clear. Across the water approached a bearded man. His hair was dark and unruly. His clothes were ragged and he was barefoot. He appeared to be walking on the surface of the water. His complexion was dark and his nose was large. He motioned for me to me come to him. I walked out on the surface of the water to where he was. We walked together to the shore where we sat down upon two large rocks. He asked me if I knew who he was. I told him that he was Jesus. Then I asked him if he knew who I was. He frowned and thought deeply for a moment. Then he said, "You are the traveler. Tell me what you have learned in your travels." I was caught totally unprepared.

"I have learned that nothing is what it appears to be...ever. I struggle with the effort to not take things personally, even when they are meant to be. Whenever a problem arises it is hard for me to look for the gift that always accompanies every challenge. It is always difficult for me to treat myself the way I would like others to treat me. And the most difficult thing of all for me to do is to forgive others so that I can finally forgive myself for my own shortcomings."

Jesus placed a gift in the palm of my hand. It looked like a large cloud-filled purple marble. He said, "Wherever you go, you will always be in the Eye of the Storm." The marble disappeared into my hand.

Hope is Not a Strategy!

When I woke up this morning and looked at the clock, it was 3:56 a.m. I wondered if something would really, actually come by my house at 4:00 o'clock in the morning. The sheep had all been counted, and recounted and were all counted out, so at 3:59 a.m., I wandered out to the curb in front of my house and waited doubtfully for 4:00 a.m. to come and go. To my surprise, that vintage red and black biplane drifted silently down out of the night sky, sliding smoothly to the slickest three point landing that a French Poodle could ever make, then taxied to my curbside, while its giant radial engine sputtered and fell silent and its shiny polished spinner slowed to a stop.

I sauntered over to the pilot and asked, "Can you take me to Toy Land?" Without a word, the big black poodle hit the starter, the engine barked loudly then rattled to life. There is no talking after a big radial engine roars to life. We were air born in less than a hundred feet but instead of climbing up into the night sky, we kept gathering speed, barely clearing the treetops and telephone poles. We continued to accelerate as telephone poles zoomed by like picket fences, then blurred into the infinity of speed and time.

The engine began to cough intermittently, as the propeller slowed and we fell out of the sky into another time and into another place, 'Toy Land.' We touched down on the dry, dusty, dirt runway from my childhood, where friends and I ventured, uninvited, to touch the delicate fabric skin and tails of a Piper Cub or a Stinson Voyager or sometimes, an ancient biplane.

The old round top hangers were still there, with the engineless yellow Cub still waiting for repair and the greasy crop duster waiting to take on another load of poison for the butterflies and the honeybees. I walked aimlessly around kicking dirt into open gopher holes which often snared the small rubber tire of an unwary pilot who strayed from the rutted dirt taxi way.

I found my old rusty, red, Radio Flyer wagon, piled high with its memories of friends from my childhood but they are all gone now, lost to time and troubles. I picked up its faded black handle and trudged down the rutted dirt road towards the asphalt that began somewhere over the hill ahead. Somehow all of my friends had fallen victim to one deadly sin or another.

Kenny fell to the siren's call. Gordon smoked

himself into the grave. Billy Joe lived to eat and died because of it. Randy was so proud, always so proud. Nothing mattered to him more than his pride. Charley made so much money, too much money, more than any man could ever spend but it was never enough, never enough. His ex-wives got it all in the end anyway. Evert killed a man out of plain meanness. He was always so angry. Nothing ever made him happy. He was just plain mad at the world. Jim Bo, well Jim Bo never changed.

When I finally made it to the pavement, I turned around and saw that everything had bounced out of my little red Radio Flyer wagon somewhere along the bumpy dirt road I had been traveling. The only thing that was still left in the little wagon was a small wooden trunk with its domed lid. I forced its rusty lock open, hoping that it might somehow be a time capsule, a relic from my past. Inside, I found a small piece of crumpled paper. On it was penciled in large upper case letters:

HOPE ALWAYS DIES LAST!'

At the End of the Rainbow

When I was little, my father would tell me there was a pot of gold at the end of the rainbow every time we saw one. That was rare living in the Sonoran Desert. Last night I was awake when it was time for the red and black biplane to pass over, so I waited out on the curb under the street light in front of our house in hopes of catching a ride. I heard the faint rumble coming from the approaching airplane. The sound dropped off sharply. I knew it was coming in for a direct approach landing. Moments later, it touched down gently at the far end of our street. The engine fell silent as the propeller spun down. The old biplane rolled silently to a stop directly in front of my driveway. I asked the pilot if he could take me to the pot of gold at the end of the rainbow. The Poodle scratched his wrinkled brow for a moment, before shaking his head up and down with an affirmative gesture. He motioned with his twirling paw for me to give the prop a pull. I signaled him with a kill sign to make sure the magneto was off before I approached the oversized wooden propeller with its tarnished brass leading edge. I pulled the propeller through slowly until one cylinder was positioned just before top dead center. I gave him the thumbs up so he could turn the magneto back on and I gave the prop a big pull. The engine popped and sputtered to life, rattling and shaking the spruce and wire structure of the rickety airframe. I clambered up into the front hole and we were off on another adventure, heading for the end of the rainbow.

It was barely 1:00 o'clock in the morning and quite dark outside. Before long it was twilight and we were flying low over what looked like Ireland, with its lush green landscape. We sat down roughly in a fairly level pasture near a dense forest, with a beautiful rainbow coming down out of the clouds just beyond. I jumped out and thanked the pilot before running into the forest in search of the rainbow's end. The forest opened abruptly at the edge of a deep, wide abyss. On the other side was a huge iron pot with the rainbow emerging from it. I had no idea how I could possibly get across the precipice. I shouted into the canyon all of the names of leprechauns that I knew. Each name echoed back to me in turn, to no avail but a rope bridge magically appeared that crossed over to the other side of the gorge. At its entrance, stood a little old leprechaun wearing an emerald green stovepipe hat and a matching bright green wool vest. I ran over to him and asked if I could cross over the chasm on his swaying rope bridge. He looked up at me, squinted his beady little eyes until they were almost closed and asked, "What is the magic word?" I replied, "I believe!" He removed his tall hat quickly and bowed so low that his nose almost touched the grass. I made my way across the swaying rope bridge to the other side and on to where the giant iron pot sat, with the rainbow bubbling up out of it.

Several leprechauns were running around the boiling pot feeding the fire at its base with dry twigs and leaves and even some pieces of old rope discarded from a worn-out bridge. Inside the huge cauldron was molten gold bubbling away, its vapors were condensing into the shimmering rainbow of colors arching across the sky towards the clouds in the distance. It was obvious that there was a pot of gold at the end of the rainbow but there was no way I could take any of the molten metal back with me.

I made my way back across the hemp rope bridge and back to my bedroom. The clock beside my bed displayed 1:20 a.m. in large red numerals. It had taken only twenty minutes to go and to come back. The only evidence left of my adventure was the brown stains on my fingers from crossing the rope bridge and the lingering smell of burning hemp rope still hanging in my bedroom.

Sugar-Plums

For the past couple of weeks the Source has been ushering me through a project that is challenging for me. Not that all of his requests aren't difficult for me to work through but this one has been especially hard for me to grasp. For the first step in this process the Source took me to a place where there was essentially nothing. He raised his right arm and in a sweeping motion from due east to southwest he said, "This is your realm. This is your domain." I didn't see anything.

I asked what he was referring to. He said that it had nothing to do with cardinal direction as in east or west or up or down or space or property but purely with reality. He left me standing there confused.

A week later he repeated the process extending the range from 120 degrees to 220 degrees, from east to northwest. Again he left me standing there alone and confused. Last night the Source swept his arm in a complete circle and said that all of it was now my realm. All of it was now my domain. Here I was capable of understanding all realities. I found that hard to believe.

Where moments before there was nothing now was filled with sugarplums dangling down on threads. He never told me anything about the sugarplums. They were very large and delicious looking. I reached out and grasped the one closest to me. The other sugarplums vanished.

A long column of pictures appeared lined up in domino fashion. They snaked their way towards me from my left side then wrapped around me and continued off to the right where they abruptly ended.

Inside each frame was a picture of me. The first one was of a newborn baby, the last one was of a very old man. There must have been a hundred of them. The one closest to me reflected me at my present age. I picked up the first picture and all of the other pictures vanished except the second photograph. In between the two, which were apparently one year apart, eleven more pictures appeared, one for each month of that first year.

I picked up the first and second photos that were taken one month apart and photos appeared for each week of my life. I picked up the first two photos and pictures of each day of that first week appeared. Then, I picked up the two photos of my first day of life and photos for each hour of that day appeared, then for each minute of that first hour. I finally understood what sugarplums really are.

They contain all of the memories of a person's life.

The Oreo Brigade

At 1:57 a.m. I went out to the front yard to catch a ride on the Night Bus. The old bus turned the corner at the end of our street a little before 2:00 o'clock. It wobbled from side to side as it slowly came down the street towards our driveway. I expected the bus to be crammed full of crazy kids jumping all over the place but when the bus driver opened the door and I climbed up the steps into the bus and looked around, the bus was completely empty. I told Brad, the bus driver, I needed to go to the twelfth attention, the source of all health and healing. As he put the bus in gear and the bus started moving, I drew my trusty 'Sword of Truth' and looked into its shiny surface to see what might actually be there in the bus. It was completely full of translucent people, all with round bald bulbous heads, staring at me through their gaunt bulging eyeballs. I asked Brad who they were. He told me they were all totally insane. He said they were all going to the twelfth attention because it was their last and only hope of becoming sane once again.

Brad stopped the bus and I jumped out through the open door and landed in a large classroom devoid of any furnishings, with a giant blackboard along one wall. This was the twelfth attention. All ninety insane souls from the night bus tumbled in after me. I had no idea what to do with all of these crazy people. I had no tools or strategies for dealing with this sort of affliction. They all stared endlessly at me with their unblinking eyes, as they crowded ever closer with their outstretched arms and grasping fingers. I needed to come up with some sort of plan and it had to be quickly.

They were all totally insane. They were all totally disconnected from physical reality. I grabbed a package of OREO cookies lying on the desk. My only thought was, "No one can resist an OREO cookie." As they reached out to grab me I placed an OREO in each grasping hand and whispered in each ear, "A taste of reality."

The delicious taste of an honest to goodness real OREO cookie melting in their mouth reconnected them to the real world and brought them back to their senses. One by one they disappeared from the twelfth attention and returned to the world of physical reality, no longer insane but completely cured by the unforgettable taste of a genuine OREO cookie.

Tsunami

It was 2:58 in the morning. I checked on the Facilitator. He had been sitting on a bench facing out overlooking the event horizon for over a week now. He sat on the left end of the bench gazing out on the event horizon. Lucky sat next to him. Sabatini sat on the other end of the bench. I stood to the side and behind the Facilitator and asked why they were all facing southeast.

He said that far out beyond the fog bank, there was a rising tide. Not merely turbulence from a troubling time but a ripple spreading out in every direction from a future event. It was a growing tide gathering strength and intensity with each passing moment. When it burst upon this small round island of sand where we now were, it would be obliterated, buried beneath the turbulent sea.

The island was composed of sand, the sands of time gathered together, created from the cumulative extrinsic mind of man. It was a vantage point from which to observe, a place from which any perception was possible.

"I suppose you want me to do something about it?" I said.

The Facilitator failed to comment. He stared silently out onto the future. It was my choice to attempt to alter the future or to allow the looming future event to destroy this island of perception crafted from the collective conscience of man.

"How could I do that? I had no idea." I waded knee deep into the calm waters and surveyed the possibilities.

I summoned a thousand Long Ships of the now, long dead Vikings, straight from Valhalla. They spread to the left and to the right in shallow water for as far as the eye could see. I stood on the prow of the central ship and signaled to furl tightly their sails and then begin the 'row' into the advancing tidal wave far out upon the future sea.

As we raced into the tidal wave I opened the domed lid of the small box. Time stood still. But the ships rowed on over the huge wave and advanced far beyond the gathering storm to the event itself that created the storm. The ships circled tightly together and began to frantically row in unison, round and round they rowed creating a growing whirlpool, faster and faster. The dead Vikings rowed frantically to forestall the event that lead to the demise of man.

The swirling vortex swallowed them all. The event would now not transpire. I walked slowly the many miles over the frozen surface of time back to where I began. I closed the lid on the small box. Time resumed.

The Facilitator looked up at me as I stood behind the three of them sitting there on the park bench on this small island of sand, looking out upon the event horizon and asked, "How did you do that?"

As I turned and walked away I said, "They owed me one!"

Me, Myself & I

My son called yesterday. He told me that he thought there was something in their swimming pool and something was also in the cave on the hill near their house. He felt there was some kind of a connection between the two separate locations and that ran right through his bedroom. It was keeping him awake at night. My son lives in Orange County. I live in Arizona. I told him that I would come over during the night and check it out and take care of whatever the issue was.

The first thing I did was to confer with the Facilitator, who always appears to me as either a huge lion or a tall, red-haired, bearded man in a pin-striped gray business suit. He was sitting on the bench by the ocean with a child about five or six years old, where he has waited for me for the last couple of weeks. He has been trying to get me up to speed, with respect to the use of the event horizon. I am getting better at seeing events from the future, before they happen. I have even had some success at preventing those events from actually occurring. I know this is basically, 'The Butterfly Effect' but it does appear to have its own element of utility.

This child is actually myself, when I was young. It was helpful to create this discontinuity in time and place in order to be able to be in two places at the same time, with two different perspectives or to be in two different times at the same place or to be in two different places and two different times simultaneously and still maintain unity of thought. The facilitator suggested that this approach would be the easiest way to become functionally competent within the event horizon.

Long ago, I asked the Facilitator what his name was. He told me that I wouldn't be able to pronounce it even if he told me what it was. I gave him a name that he thought was appropriate, and we left it at that. For personal reasons, I will refer to him as the Facilitator. I asked him if he would mind going with me, simply because I had no idea what I would be encountering. He agreed to accompany me on this project. I didn't want the child to tag along because I felt I wouldn't be able to look after him adequately while engaging something totally unknown. So, I took him into Never Land for safekeeping. There, we had a recent visitor, Baldwin, whom I thought might be willing to entertain this child, while the Facilitator and I took care of our business in California. Our new guest was Baldwin the dwarf. I was surprised by his response.

Baldwin felt that he should accompany us on this quest and that we should bring the child along with us. He said that dwarfs have powerful magic, and he vowed that he would keep the child safe. His final argument was that there was strength in numbers. "Never go alone, and never go unprepared," he said. How do you convince a five hundred year old dwarf that he can't go on an adventure or that he can't adequately look after a child who is six years old, especially when he was right about there being strength in numbers and always being prepared. We went together to the bridge that goes into Never Land. I left them there to wait for me, while I assembled the rest of our expeditionary party.

Two of the most powerful characters I know are the Lion and the Other. The Other is something only an exceptional sorcerer can create, and then only with the use of deep magic. The Other is extremely powerful and indestructible. It is a luminous double of the sorcerer. The Other is the alter ego of the sorcerer. I went to the secret place where the Other resides, updated its memory so that it was identical to mine, then brought the Other and the Lion back to the bridge to rendezvous with Baldwin and the six year old child.

I took them to the portal that would transport all of us to California. Everyone held hands, and together, we walked through that door and into my son's back yard. It was immediately apparent that something was in his swimming pool. The pool is twelve or fourteen feet deep, unlike our play pool in Tucson, which is only seven feet deep. There, against the east side of the pool, on the deep end, a luminous something glowed brightly beneath the surface. Baldwin rushed forward, turned and shouted excitedly, "It's the Oakenthor. I've heard that it exists, but I don't know anyone who has ever actually seen it."

I had no idea what an Oakenthor was. "Tell me what it is, so we can figure out what to do with it," I said? Baldwin told us that the Oakenthor is a solid gold Oak tree that has magical powers, and that it is one of the most sacred of sacred things to dwarfs. "Well," I said, "That thing must weigh a ton. I'll have the Other get it out of the water for us, then we have to figure out some way to get it back home to Tucson."

The Other immediately jumped into the pool and lifted the Oakenthor out of the water and placed it on the Saltillo tile deck. The child ran over to the solid gold oak tree that was at least eight feet tall and grabbed onto its trunk with both of his hands. The Oakenthore immediately shrank to the size of a small egg in the palm of the child's hand. Lucky, the small child nonchalantly put it into his pocket and rejoined us without uttering a single word.

Well, so much for that problem. The next challenge was the shadowy tube. It passed from the pool directly into my son's bedroom at the end of the house. It was about four inches in diameter. We followed the tube as it went right through the house, then out the other side, then up the hill, and into the cave.

As we entered, the right side of the cave opened up onto the hillside of a picturesque country setting. Baldwin lurched forward. "That's my village, that's where I live. There's my house by the big tree," he said, as he dragged us down the hillside into his world.

Baldwin introduced us to his neighbors, his friends, and his family. He insisted that we come into his house and sit for dinner with him at his table. I passed through the doorway without ducking my head but just, barely so. Once we were inside Baldwin's house, we made our way to the table. It was in the center of the largest room in the house. It was like a huge picnic table, with heavy benches down each side and a three-legged stool at each end. The tabletop was ancient. It was at least four inches thick, maybe even six inches thick, made of solid wood that was so old and so weathered that our plates wobbled on its hand-hewn surface. The only utensils were hand-carved wooden spoons. No napkins and no glasses were visible. Rough tankards were passed around. They were filled with the dwarf's favored brew. It was something like the moonshine of my own youth, liquid fire almost impossible to swallow. The only food was a very large platter of boiled root vegetables and loaves of dark brown bread as hard as the table itself. This was what Baldwin described as their celebratory fare, the feast of his return as a dwarf, not as a Shebob.

With that first swallow, I gasped, coughed, cleared my throat, and insisted, that we had urgent unfinished business to complete and must depart immediately. We thanked all of the dwarfs for their hospitality and escaped back into our own world, our own time, and our own dimension, but not before promising to return again soon.

The next day I asked my son what the status of his house was. He said that everything was gone including the strange tube that ran through his bedroom connecting the pool with the cave on the hill, and everything was once again back to normal. I ventured into Never Land to check the area where Baldwin had been camping out, for any forgotten items. There, under the trunk of a fallen tree, was the pipe Baldwin forgot to take with him on our adventure into the unknown. I knew then, that I would have to return that pipe to Baldwin sometime, but not today.

Oakenthor

After I returned from de-activating the portal transport device, I had a long discussion with the Oakenthor. We communicated for over an hour telepathically. This is what was shared with me.

I asked Oakenthor what it was doing in my son's swimming pool in the first place. It said that it always looked for places with very high energy densities, and that his swimming pool was packed with the right kind of energy.

Several months ago, my son was injured in an accident. He had transitioned out of his wheel chair and was using crutches. He was beginning physical therapy, but he was not yet able to put his full weight on his injured feet. Exercising in the pool was advocated by his orthopedic surgeon. I took it upon myself to transfer vast amounts of energy into the water itself, in hopes that this would speed my son's recovery.

Not long after that, two Mallard ducks took up residency in his swimming pool. They spent every night there, then left to forage for food during the day. Pooping ducks was not helpful to the healing process, in my opinion. It took several attempts to get the ducks to leave, before I was successful. They were determined to stay in their newfound heated swimming pool, for the winter. The high energy density in the swimming pool was what attracted Oakenthor there.

Oakenthor's first memories were those of sitting in front of a campfire across from a man at night who was clothed in animal skins. His footwear was composed of animal furs held in place with leather strips wound around the feet, up the ankles, around the calves, and tied just below the knees. The fur sides of these skins were on the inside, and the outside was exposed leather. The man's hands were covered with animal skins with the fur also on the insides and all of the fingers sticking out through five holes punched in the skins. These crude gloves were also kept in place with leather thongs. His knees were bare. The rest of his body was covered with more fur skins held in place with a leather sash. In the background, there was snow everywhere.

Oakenthor said that most of his existence had been spent in one enclosure after another, only the hands that reached in to retrieve it changed. Most of the hands were those of men but a few were those of women. The last hands that retrieved Oakenthor were those of a woman. Her left hand held a white dove, and her right hand held Oakenthor. She faced east and released both at the same time into the rising sun. From there Oakenthor ended up in my son's swimming pool.

It seems that those individuals who had possession of Oakenthor only used it to injure or eliminate other people or things. The Oakenthor has the ability to turn matter into energy. The energy transfer from the thing being attacked by Oakenthor looks similar to electricity, thus its glowing golden color. The Oakenthor appears as a golden oak tree, though it is neither a tree, nor is it made of gold. The object being attacked sizzles and sputters as it is being converted into pure energy that is then absorbed back into the Oakenthor.

An interesting perspective shared by the Oakenthor was that it never felt imprisoned. To the contrary, those who used the Oakenthor themselves became imprisoned by their own growing dependency upon the Oakenthor. Dependency on others, imprisons oneself. Self-reliance sets one free.

The Lion's Gait

I haven't been allowed into the third attention since I have been wearing the Oakenthor on a silk string around my neck, under my shirt, and out of sight. The Oakenthor was created by a powerful sorcerer, who utilized deep magic, somewhere, in the long forgotten past. The Oakenthor has unbelievable powers but its only function is to destroy. I had been unable to figure out what to do with it. Dealing with deep magic is terribly difficult. Leaving a powerful device like the Oakenthor untended would be unthinkable.

Last night I asked the Facilitator, who actually has a name, if there was anything he wanted to tell me or to show me or if there was any place he wanted to take me. He was standing next to me on the sandy beach near the event horizon, wearing his familiar pinstriped gray suit with its pastel tie. He thought for a moment then, he said that he wanted to take me for a walk. He told me not to look down, transformed himself into a very large male lion, and told me to hang on tightly to his hairy mane.

We took off at a fast pace, not quite jogging but I was walking very quickly to keep up with the lion's gait. Periodically he reminded me not to look down. After a while, my body moved on its own, like a distance runner on a runner's high. At first I could see my body and the lion moving swiftly towards the West, as I floated upward into darkness, then I was alone in a moving meditation. Darkness and silence were my companions.

From the darkness appeared something familiar, something I had not seen in some time, the Tree of Life, a beautiful luminescent tree with shimmering leaves of light. I made my way over to it, sat down and leaned my back against its rigid trunk and closed my eyes. I began to hear the rustling of its leaves by some invisible wind. The sounds were not those of leaves but the tinkle of small glass, ceramic, and metal objects. When I opened my eyes, the leaves had all been transformed into small luminescent replicas of all kinds of things.

The tinkling sounds encouraged me onward, as I climbed upward into the tree's branches, brushing against innumerable small glowing symbols, until I was far out on a branch, where I removed the small golden oak tree on its silken string from around my neck and tied the Oakenthor securely to an empty spot on a strong stem. I made my way back along the branch and climbed down out of the Tree of Life, looked back up at the golden little oak tree dancing there in the invisible winds, along with all of the other objects and then, in an instant, I was standing next to the man in the pinstriped gray suit on the sandy beach.

Neither of us spoke. We sat down together on the park bench, which was facing south, towards the event horizon and we gazed out onto the smooth empty sea in silence.

After a while, I stood up and walked away and into the third attention. There, complete darkness surrounded me. In the distance I saw a single oak tree, standing alone on the top of a small hill. I walked over to the beautiful old oak tree and sat down under its spreading branches. I closed my eyes and crossed my legs.

I knew that the circle had been closed. The task had been done. The deep magic had been broken and the Oakenthor was free.

The Lion's Gate had closed.

Stilt Man

A couple of nights ago I awoke and checked the time displayed on the clock next to my bed. It showed 3:33 a.m. I jumped out of bed and ran out in front of our driveway and sat down in the middle of the street and waited. I faced in all four cardinal directions at the same time. I wanted to see what might come by at this time in the morning. Out of thin air a man on stilts materialized and walked towards me. He stopped right in front of me and motioned for me to stand up. When I did so, he handed me a pair of stilts and motioned for me to put them on.

After I secured the stilts to my legs the stranger helped me stand up. I asked him how to use them. He said, "Don't fall down." I thought that was a dumb answer. He thought mine was a dumb question. He said they were magic stilts and they could take me anywhere I chose to go. After a lengthy demonstration, the stranger told me the stilts were a gift and I should use them wisely. He then proceeded to walk right through me and became a part of me.

Later that night I asked the Source about the stilts, the stranger and his disappearing act. The Source said that he thought I was ready to use the magic in these stilts, so he sent the stranger to deliver them. He added that the stranger was actually a part of myself. He said the stilts made me stand taller than any person. This gave me a different perspective of everything.

Everyone would look up at me. I would look down at them but I should never look down on them. Everyone would look up to me and ask me to do things for them. I should always do the things that I could for others but I should never ask them to do anything for me or expect anything in return.

It is true everything does look different now that I see things from a different point of view.

The Plank

The other night the Source asked me to walk with him. We walked along side by side for a while until we came to a narrow, wooden walkway. It was less than three feet wide. It was more like twenty-eight inches or so. The Source told me this was 'The Plank,' not a plank but 'The Plank.' It could be compared to the walkway used for boarding a ship or for disembarking from a ship or a boat.

In this case he compared it to "Walking the Plank," on perhaps a pirate-ship. He was attempting to explain a concept to me as an allegory, the allegory of one 'walking the plank.' This is how he explained it to me as I was walking on this narrow, wooden plank and he was walking beside me on what seemed to me to be nothing at all.

"When you get on a ship it is uncertain whether

you will survive your journey on not. So, a ship in essence represents uncertainty. When you leave the ship and get back on dry land you are again uncertain as to what awaits you upon your return. Therefore, it also is uncertainty. But if you are 'Walking the Plank' on a pirate-ship you know that the plank ends and you know with certainty that the ocean awaits you and it is filled with hungry sharks that are waiting for you to be their dinner. So, the plank between the ship and dry land in that sense is certainty while the ship and dry land are both rife with uncertainty. Now, I want you to close your eyes and 'walk the plank.'"

As we continued walking he said, " You noticed that I walked beside you while you walked on the plank but where I was walking there was no plank. Now I want you to open your eyes and tell me what you see."

I looked down and there was no plank. I was standing on a small oval shaped stepping-stone. Each time I took a step, another oval stepping-stone appeared. The Source turned to me and said, "As long as you walk with me, there will always be a stepping stone for you to walk upon. There will always be certainty for you."

Dream Portal

I never knew that such a place as this actually

existed; apparently it does. In the last week I have been there five times. I'm not yet sure exactly how this process works but I'm trying to figure it out.

The Source escorted me to this Dream Portal three times in the last week. Subsequently, I have been there twice on my own. The first time I was there, the Source asked me what I saw. We seemed to be floating above a dividing line between two separate places. The dividing line was like a fence observed from directly above. Both sides were very difficult for me to make out but one side did appear to be different than the other side. Each time I returned the two sides appeared more clearly and was more distinct. On the third visit a triangular shape appeared on the right side of the line of demarcation. Nothing was ever visible on the left side of the separation, which was oriented vertically. I was positioned above, looking down upon it.

The point of the acute angle of the triangle rested against the line of demarcation. The side opposite this acute angle was absent creating a funnel shape with the ends of the two remaining sides extending out and away from the line of demarcation. I really had no idea what this place was or how it functioned. After the Source saw that I could return to this very spot on my own he told me what it was and how it worked.

He said that the world of the living was on the left side of the demarcation and the spirit world of the dead was on the right side of the fence or curtain that was the line of demarcation. Non-living spirits could enter the open side of the triangle and bring messages and attach them to this fence. Apparently the point where the acute angle touched the fence or curtain, spirits could attach their messages for the living. The living could receive these messages from the dearly departed from this Dream Portal while they were asleep and in the dream state.

This could be analogous to a prayer wall or a wall where people leave messages for others to hopefully someday receive while dreaming.

Confidence Window

A couple of nights ago the Source showed me a very large picture frame. It was four feet in height and seven feet in width. He referred to it as a window. He said that this window would allow an observer to view any event in the past, present or future with a degree of certainty. He left it at that for me to try and figure out how to use it. It was not a window as we might think of a window. It was a large frame for a picture suspended in mid-air with no picture and no glass in it. You could look right through it and see everything on the other side. I worked on this frame project for quite a while but it was obvious to me that I was getting nowhere.

Last night the Source took me back to where the window was located and explained to me how it worked. On the left side of the frame a little more than half way up from the bottom was a small invisible door that opened out and to the left. There was some buttons and a display behind this door. Here you were supposed to enter the degree of certainty in percentage points that you desired.

On the opposite side of the frame there was another secret door that opened to the right and exposed more buttons and another display. Here you were supposed to enter the date and time of the event that you wanted to observe.

On the top of the window frame in the center, there was a third secret door that opened upwards. Here you were supposed to enter the name of the person and the specific event in question.

The fourth secret door was located in the center of the bottom frame of the window. It opened downward and had only three options from which you could choose. The top choice was the reality of that person associated with that particular happening or event. The second choice was your own personal reality or point of view. The third choice was the actual reality of that event.

I tried it out a few times. It seemed to work fairly well but the higher the degree of certainty you requested, the more difficult the task is to complete.

Black Door

Last night I was talking with the Source in 'The Place.' He asked me to recharge there with the maximum amount of energy that I could because he wanted to show me something afterwards. When I finished recharging he wanted me to completely clear my mind of any thoughts and then to stop my internal dialog. At that point he outlined a black rectangle with wide, bold, lines. He asked me what I thought it was. I told him that I didn't know. He then proceeded to fill the outline in completely. It looked like a large upright rectangle to me. He said, "This is a door."

It had no hinges and no doorknob or handle. He re-iterated, "This is a door. This is your door. Only you can open this door. Only you can use this door. It will take you anywhere, to any place, to any time, to any reality, to any universe."

Then he presented me with a key on a gold chain and placed it around my neck. Being the skeptic that I am I asked where I should put the key since the door had no lock and no knob, no hinges and no handle. And then I asked what if someone took the key away from me. At that time the gold chain and the key itself sank deep into my chest and neck and the Source said, "You are the key. You and only you can open this door to anywhere." I was left standing alone in front of the large black door with no visible hinges, handles or locks.

Dealer's Deck

As I left 'The Place' last night, the Source asked me to walk with him. We walked a short ways until we came upon a very small table for two with a deck of cards placed face down on one side. The Source asked me to sit down and two chairs appeared out of thin air.

We sat down at the dealer's table. The Source spread the cards smoothly in an ark across the table with one movement of his hand. He then asked me to pick a card. I picked one from the middle and turned it over. It was a Queen of Spades. He asked me to pick another card. I chose another card and turned it over. It was the Jack of Diamonds. Again he wanted me to pick another card. I picked another card and turned it over. It was the Ace of Hearts. One final time the Source asked me to pick another card. I did so and it turned out to be the three of Clubs.

The Source leaned back in his chair and asked me what I thought of the cards I had chosen. I looked at them and looked back at him and said that I didn't think anything of the cards. The Source told me that those were my cards. That was my hand and they represented my life. He then turned all of the other cards over facing up. They were all blank. There was nothing on any of them. He waited for me to give him an answer. I said that I had no idea what the cards meant. I knew nothing about the cards.

The Source then elaborated. The Queen of Spades

represents the women in your life. They have always come first before anything else. The Jack of Diamonds represents you, a jack-of-all-trades, a diamond in the rough. The Ace of Hearts represents the love you have for all creatures, great and small. The three of Clubs are the three doors that wait for you just outside 'The Place.' The door to the left is the Door of Prophecy. The door in the center is the Door to the Oracle and the door to your right is the Door to the connection between all things, past, present & future. These cards represent your life. They are your cards. This is your hand and you have chosen to play them.

The Source vanished. I picked up the deck of blank cards and turned them over. On each card was the face of a woman, all of the many women in my life who have had a hand in creating who I am and what I am capable of doing. On the very first card was a picture of my mother.

Poker Chips

Last night I sat down across from the Source at a narrow card table. He was completely surrounded by a mountain of different colored poker chips. There were ten different colors; Gold, silver, white, red, yellow, blue, green, purple, orange and black. In front of me was a deck of cards. I had all of the cards and the

Source had all of the chips.

I had no idea what sort of game the Source had in mind for me to play, so I asked questions about the type of game and what the point of playing was. I asked about the valuation of the different colored chips. He said the value of each chip varied depending on the person and on the situation but he never provided me with any specifics.

I asked the Source about the cards, which were all face down in a stack. He said they were my cards. They represented my life and I had to play them. I asked how many cards were in the deck. He said that the number of cards depended on how old I was. The older I was, the fewer cards were left to play. When I turned them over, they were all blank.

I asked how the game was to be played. He told me to think carefully and then tell him the ten things I wanted most from this life in their descending order of importance to me, not to others in my life. I gave this game some serious thought and this is what I asked for:

Good health. Without good health, nothing else matters. I gave the Source my first card and he gave me a gold chip.

Good vision. Without the ability to see life is very challenging. I gave the Source my second card and he gave me a silver chip.

Good food. Without good healthy food you will be sick. I gave the Source my third card and he gave me a white chip.

Love. Without love nothing has meaning. I gave the Source my fourth card and he gave me a red chip.

Clean air. Without clean air every living thing will suffer. I gave the Source my fifth card and he gave me a yellow chip.

Healthy oceans. Without clean oceans all life will suffer. I gave the Source my sixth card and he gave me a blue chip.

Verdant planet Earth. Without green plants, animals will die. I gave the Source my seventh card and he gave me a green chip.

No debilitating pain. Chronic pain makes life very challenging. I gave the source my eighth card and he gave me a purple chip.

Peace on Earth. Without peace there is suffering and death. I gave the source my ninth card and he gave me an orange chip.

The 'good' death. Death awaits us all but not severe pain. I gave the Source my tenth card and he gave me a black chip.

The Source said to me, "You chose wisely" and everything vanished.

Your Train

I was talking with the Source last night. He said to me, "Your life is like a train. You started in one place and have traveled to all kinds of other places hauling all sorts of things that you delivered and then moved on and on until you will finally make your last delivery at your last stop. You don't get to choose all the many different things you carry. You don't get to choose where they are dropped off. Your schedule is not your own. Your destinations are not of your choosing. The grade is sometimes steep. The weather is sometimes harsh. The track is not always straight. The load is sometimes damaged. The load is sometimes lost. It is often not on time and rarely meets the expectations of others. You didn't get to choose when your journey began. You will just keep going and going and going, until you finally run out of track."

Barriers

The other night when I asked the Source what was next on his agenda for me to do, he said that he wanted me to look straight ahead and go on until I hit the barrier. He said, "Don't look down, don't look up, don't look to your left, don't look to your right and most important of all don't turn back or look behind you." Then, he vanished. I was in what I thought was the "Place of Emptiness."

It was a real challenge for me to not look up or down, to my right or to my left and most difficult of all was to not look back. Eventually I was able to keep my attention focused straight ahead. He told me to begin and end with my left foot. " Start and stop with your left foot. Stay on the path. Stay on task."

I looked down and there was no path. A steppingstone would appear with each step I took. The first barrier for me was to look straight ahead, then and only then did things begin to appear. I moved through them. I moved beyond them one by one. First there were a series of things, then a series of issues all of which symbolized a personal obstacle, a personal impediment for me that I had to overcome. Finally an image of the Source appeared. I walked through it. Then an image of the Devil appeared. I walked through that also. The final barrier was a thin yellow plastic ribbon stretched across my path, fluttering in an invisible wind. Written on it in large black, block letters was "The Unknown." That stopped me in my path.

I moved up to it and attached what Sorcerers call "The Will" onto it. The ribbon stopped fluttering. The 'Will' is an extension, which protrudes from the umbilical area of a sorcerer's abdomen. It is very powerful and can be used to accomplish many amazing things. When I moved, the yellow ribbon moved with me. When I stopped, the yellow ribbon of the "Unknown" stopped as well. I had finally reached the "Barrier," my barrier, "The Unknown."

The next time I talked with the Source, he asked me if I had reached the "Barrier." When I told him that I had reached the barrier of the "Unknown," he was pleased and stated that the Unknown was the final barrier for everyone.

My next assignment was to go beyond the barrier of the "Unknown." It was a strange maneuver for me. I released my "Will" from the yellow ribbon, spun around counter-clockwise and did a backflip over the yellow ribbon, then re-connected to it from the other side leaving the "Unknown" behind me.

The Source said to me, "You are now immersed completely in the Unknown. You are now within the world of the Wizard, the realm of the Buddha. You now have access to this vastness of the Unknown, the Unknowable. The journey of the wizard involves the transformation of the Unknowable into the Known."

The Source told me it was time for me to re-visit the twenty-six strings now that I had moved on beyond the barrier of the "Unknown."

In order to get there I would have to travel back in time to the moment of the creation, the 'Big Bang,' when God created everything out of nothingness. I asked the Source exactly what was I supposed to do when I got there. He said, "Bear witness to the creation of all that is from the vastness of the void."

The Eagle's Beak

Last night I went back three times through the 'Black Door' to a point just before the 'Big Bang' of creation transpired, to witness its unfolding so that I might locate the origins of these twenty-six strings that the Source wants me to visit. Each time the event looked the same. It was very different than I thought it would be. All of creation spewed out of nothingness like a giant twisted rope unraveling as it spun around its long axis. Each of these strings had a round illuminated sphere at its head. They were attached at different points all along this unraveling rope. Everything was created out of nothingness and spewed out from the edge of the void. All of the parts of the universe were moving in one direction. It was not like an exploding bomb, expanding out from its center. Each string was connected at its origin by a large tube. Everything else was attached to the origin by a thin rope or thread.

I thought my journey here to bear witness to the creation was a singularity but it immediately became apparent that this is what the Sorcerer, Don Juan, refers to as 'The Eagle's Beak' in Carlos Castaneda's 'Teachings of Don Juan.' Everything and everyone is ultimately attached by a thread or string to the 'Eagles Beak.' Sorcerers, Buddha and holy men have obviously been witness to this creation long before me.

For me, God was the Source. God was also the eagle

and this was the 'Eagle's Beak.'

God's gift to each of us is our life. The Gift we give to God in return is, how we live that life.

Quantum Space

The Source told me that he wanted to take me to another place. I routinely go to what he refers to as 'the place' to recharge my energy supply that I use during awareness transport. Awareness transport is what allows me to go where I go and do what I do. This allows me to travel throughout time and places and realities that have time. Time travel and ergo, travel to other places, requires vast amounts of energy. Every night I go to 'the place' to restore the energy consumed during these traveling activities.

Quantum Space has no time but is filled with infinite energy and infinite possibility. The only entrance into Quantum Space is through the 'Eagles Beak.' In Quantum Space there are no 'Singularities.' The energy and possibilities in Quantum Space apply to and are associated with the 'Will.' God used his 'Will' to create the universe from 'Nothingness,' for in Quantum Space nothing exists. Quantum Space is where God exists. Quantum Space is separate from the 'Place of Emptiness' and 'The Void.' The 'Eagles Beak' is the location where the engine of creation injects time into what was dreamed up and energized by the 'Will' of God, creating physical reality.

In physical reality God is a singularity, but a singularity with many facets. To the Hindu each facet is described as a separate and different God. In Quantum Space there are no singularities only infinite energy and infinite possibility where God's 'Will' funnels energy and possibility through the 'Eagles Beak' and engine of creation manifesting as physical reality. In Quantum Space God is infinite and not a singularity. This is where he has taken me to tap into this unlimited energy and possibility with the expectation that I can master the use of the 'Will.'

Eye-D-Us

Once you have been to a place it is always possible to find your way back there. The next night I returned to the 'Quantum Space.' Since there was supposed to be nothing there in that space except infinite possibility and infinite energy I expected to find nothing there. But, to my surprise there were eyes everywhere. Some of them were in pairs. Some of them were individuals. All of them were staring straight at me. I asked the Source what was going on and where all of these eyes had come from.

The Source reminded me that only my sense of

awareness was there…nothing else. And, that the eyes were gateways to ideas. Every idea that ever was or ever will be resides there in Quantum Space, as infinite possibilities.

I returned the next night to Quantum Space to as they say, 'Give it a go.' My intent was to create interest in the books I have recently published. At first there was nothing, then a single eye appeared from the side. I was looking at a right eye from its side, no face and no head, just a single eye. The first challenge for me was to rotate the eye ninety-degrees, so that I could enter it. As I passed through the pupil I emerged into a place shrouded in dense fog. Out of the fog emerged a tall, thin, attractive young woman, dressed in a floor length white, silk gown carrying a bouquet of white flowers in her right hand. Her hair was dark-brown, almost black. It was long and held back behind her ears by a tiara or dia-dema. When she was close to me she held up the bouquet of white rose buds. There were at least a couple dozen of them, perhaps even twenty-six…one for each of the twenty-six strings. Out of the center of the bouquet a single red rose emerged. It blossomed and in its center was a single gold egg. I removed the gold egg with my Will, imbued it with Intent, then took it over to the back side of the Eagle's Beak and slipped it gently into the Stream of Consciousness as it spewed out into physical reality.

At that moment twenty-six faces encircled me. They were all the same face of the Source. They were pleased. They said that this is where I would enter into each string one at a time from here in Quantum Space where everything was done with the 'Will' by Intent where the only currency is emotion. Their parting admonition was, "Beware the Dark Side."

Knower's Circle

Last night I went back to the Quantum Space to talk with the Source. He introduced me there to the Knower's Circle. It consisted of twenty-six busts of what appeared to me to be identical replications of himself arranged completely around me in a circle. The Source told me these twenty-six talking heads represented each of the twenty-six strings of reality emanating from the Eagle's Beak, the Engine of Creation. Each of them was slightly different from the others with respect to their appearance. Each of them knew all about their particular stream of reality and each of them was the only point of entry into that specific reality and also the only exit point back out from that reality.

In Quantum Space there are certain basic fundamental concepts in play. On the surface they may sound superficial and simple but they can and do take a lifetime to appreciate and truly comprehend. Here we are talking about the concept of 'Knowing.' Each of you has probably had an experience of not knowing something one moment and then suddenly in an instant, knowing it the next moment to be true, as though you have always known it to be true. 'Knowing' is not knowledge based on learning. Its origin has nothing to do with your beliefs or religion or education or intelligence. It is universal truth, universal reality, universal perspective.

Also at play in Quantum Space are, the 'Will' and 'Intent' as well as 'Emotion' the only currency of change. Quantum Space is God's Domain from which everything is created and sustained. This is the place of infinite energy and infinite possibility. Nothing physical exists in this space. The 'Will' is the only instrument with which one can 'Do' anything. It is not physical. It is the instrument of 'Change.'

'Intent' is the pattern, the mold, the entirety of what is intended. As an analogy, it could be compared to DNA as the entirety of the plan of an organism. But in actuality, 'Intent' also includes the what, the when and the why and the where of for any creation.

In unison all twenty-six of the Knowers responded, " Beware the Dark Side."

Fifth String

Last night I again returned to Quantum Space to continue my efforts to investigate String Theory. I didn't know where to start. I thought our own string was perhaps number three because we have three dimensions or perhaps number four because we also have time but I was informed that our string is actually the fifth string. Then I wanted to know which one of the twenty-six busts was the entry point into that fifth string. The fifth bust identified itself. It was straight in front of me. Before I entered, the bust informed me that with this and only with this string I would not have to come back out of it through the Eagles Beak because this was the string in which I already existed and was functional and familiar with. It would be possible for me to exit into any time or place. At the time, this seemed like a good thing. Before I entered, the fifth bust informed me that going through the Engine of Creation and the Eagle's Beak would be a very rough ride and I might not survive the experience or I might not return at all and possibly end up physically in a different time or a different place and not be able to get back to my original time or place of origin. The bust also stated that only the pure of heart and true of spirit with a clear conscience would have any chance of surviving this transit. I should also have all my personal affairs in good order. That was enough for me to postpone the journey, at least for the moment.

I was Thinking

I was thinking that this process might lend itself to physical travel in time and space. What I do, is to travel as pure awareness not as a physical entity. It is possible to materialize in a different time or different place, by 'Doing,' that is what sorcerers do.

On the other hand, time does not exist in Quantum Space. So when you pass through the 'Engine of Creation' and are injected back into time and into the stream of consciousness, you probably acquire a physical form of some kind. If so, what form would that be and where in time could it be placed. You might have your prior physical form or perhaps an alternate form. You might be re-situated in current time or a different time as well as a different place. Then, how would you get back to where and when and who you were. It might also be possible to intentionally go physically into a different time or a different place and in a different form or as a different person. I was just thinking about it, before I actually go and do it.

I was Talking

Last night I was talking with the Source. During the course of our conversation the question of, "What was the point of....? came up regarding several things that have transpired.

There was a time in the past, before I began to write these things down, that I would share my adventures with my assistants in the morning at the office and then pretty much forget them. One of my assistants, who has worked with me for thirty years, kept insisting that I write them down. I would always tell her, that it was too much trouble. Eventually I acquiesced and began to record some of them, maybe five percent, at most. This eventually led to the creation of several books. The first of those books was "Coincidental Journey." I asked the Source what the real point was for that book. He said, "It was your introduction into the process of re-incarnation."

The next book published after that was "Robin." It was a book that I wrote in 1996, more than twenty years ago. It is a book in archaic English, a book of Elizabethan Poetry that I transcribed for a person who was in Purgatory and answered to the name of Robin. Her real name was Sonja Sjorgensen. She died before the age of eighteen from fever. I promised Robin that I would publish her story before she turned twenty-one on November the eleventh, two thousand and seventeen. I made a promise to Robin and I kept that promise. This book is also about re-incarnation.

The next book I wrote was "Untold Story." The Source told me last night for the first time that the purpose for that book was to prevent the start of nuclear war with North Korea by the intervention of "the Hammer."

The point of the next book "Wizardling" was to give me the tools not only of the Sorcerer but also those of a wizard.

The book "Vision Quest" was intended to provide me with a gateway to the twenty-six realities that make up String Theory. My 'Vision Quest' was intended to get me through those barriers created by things and then the barriers created by beliefs, concepts and perceptions, all the way to the ultimate barrier that is the Unknown. The challenge for me then became to go beyond the barrier of the unknown to reach Quantum Space, where nothing exists but infinite energy and infinite possibilities. My task became to make the unknowable knowable, the unknown known, the impossible possible.

Early in the morning I returned to Quantum Space, where nothing physical exists, in search of an idea on how to increase public interest in the books I write. I was looking for an eye in Quantum Space. Out of the fog of uncertainty emerged that same tall female figure that presented me with the golden egg. She brought a single candle in a brass holder. She presented it to me and lit it. She said, "This is the light the whole world will see. Place it in the front window so everyone can see it." I asked who she was.

She said she was my Guardian Angle and she had always watched over me. Then, she vanished leaving me holding the lighted candle, which I placed in the front window of our house, for all the world to see.

I asked the Source about the angel and how she

could be in Quantum Space where angels never go and about the candle itself being there in Quantum Space. I thought that was impossible. The Source said that only I could speak the angel's name, no one else but he never told me her name. He said that those things were impossible but somehow, I had managed to do them anyway.

Triad Foundation

Last night I returned to Quantum Space seeking an idea on how to more effectively promote the books I have written. Out of the fog emerged my Guardian Angel, that tall attractive female. In her hand she held a golden triangle. She presented it to me and told me I could create a solid triad foundation with it upon which I could build a successful strategy for the sale and distribution of the books I write. What triad?

For one leg of the triad I used the Gold Egg. For the second leg of the triad I used the Ring of Truth. For the third leg of the triad I used the gold triangle, which allows me to see future outcomes. Then I threw in the bouquet of roses.

The next night I returned to Quantum Space to advance my creation of the Triad. I wasn't sure how to precisely structure it. My Guardian Angel returned.

She presented me with an ornate, filigreed, silver cross about six by nine inches in size. I thanked her and asked what it was for. She told me it would protect me from the evil that I would encounter on my journey into the twenty-six strings. I asked how I should structure the triad. She said, " Put the Circle of Truth on the bottom. Inscribe the Triangle of Outcomes inside the circle. Place an eye in the center of the triangle with the golden egg as the pupil. Surround the symbol with the roses and release it into the intake of the engine of creation and it will become physical reality." My Guardian Angel showed me where the intake was. I also placed the silver cross into the intake and it instantly materialized as a giant cross hovering horizontally over my house. It was now time for me to begin my exploration of the twenty-six strings of String Theory.

Glossary

Adept – A term used by Buddhists when referring to a seer or person with the gift of prophecy.

Aru – The keeper of Dream Time

Black Door – The tool given to me that allows me to travel to any place or reality in the past, present or future in an instant and return safely.

Confidence Window – A windowless, window frame, that can be used to determine the degree of certainty of past, present or future events.

Dream Portal – The point analogous to a prayer wall where the dead can leave messages for the living to hopefully someday be retrieved by the living while they are dreaming.

Dreamscape – The place or places where dreams are created and transpire.

Dream Time – The place Aborigine's believe is real and permanent as opposed to our own here and now.

Dream Walker – A person who can materialize and function fully within the Dream Scape.

Eagle's Beak – That point at which all things are connected to the creator and to creation.

Engine of Creation – That mechanism by which time is injected into something imbuing it with life and physicality.

Event Horizon – That point in time and space where things will occur or happen.

Gazing – The art of acquiring information about anything by moving one's awareness into that object or thing to extract it.

Global Perspective – The ability to simultaneously see in all directions at the same time.

Intent – The sum totality of everything that makes up or constitutes that particular thing.

Knower's Circle – The twenty-six talking heads that represent each of the twenty-six strings of reality that emanate from the Eagle's Beak. Each of them knows all about their particular stream of reality and each of them is the only point of entry into that specific reality and also the only exit point back out of that reality.

Ligot – "Ligot is that uncontrollable rage arising from primitive minds of jungle tribesmen when they encounter a tragic loss in combination with extreme fear of the unknown.

Other –Is a luminous double of a sorcerer, which the sorcerer created. It is extremely powerful and indestructible. It is an extension of sorcerer's will and It cannot be injured or killed.

Pale – The gossamer fabric curtain, which separates the world of the living from the world of the dead.

Place of Emptiness – The place where nothing exists.

Quantum Space -Every idea that ever was or ever will be resides in Quantum Space as infinite possibilities. Quantum Space has no time but is filled with an infinite amount of energy and infinite possibilities. The only entrance into Quantum Space is through the 'Eagles Beak.' In Quantum Space there are no 'Singularities.' The energy and possibilities in Quantum Space can only be manipulated with the 'Will.' God used his 'Will' to create the universe from 'Nothingness,' for in Quantum Space nothing exists. Quantum Space is where God exists. Quantum Space is separate from the 'Place of Emptiness' and 'The

Void.' It is located between the void and the place of emptiness. The 'Eagles Beak' is the location where the engine of creation injects time into what was dreamed up and energized by the 'Will' of God, creating physical reality.

Rememberings – Memories from the past brought to life and used to alter the present.

Robin – Ghost-writer to Shakespeare.

Shape Shifter– An individual that can change their physical appearance and nature, within the dreamscape or within physical reality.

'The Crack in the Earth' – That place where two parallel universes are connected, or are in very close proximity to each other, i.e. 'The Crack in the Earth' which is a narrow canyon with vertical walls of solid rock on either side separated by a deep narrow bottomless crevasse. On each side of the canyon there is a narrow trail cut into the solid rock not more than three feet wide.

The Place – A location filled with infinite energy. The place where I go every night to restore my supply.

The Source – God

The Triangle of Outcomes – The triangle inscribed in the Circle of Truth.

The Void – The place where nothing physical is located. It is the only entrance to Quantum Space. It is vacant but all things originate there.

Wararies – Marauders that consume ones memories, dreams and even ones personal dreamscape.

Will – A physical extension of one self that is used to manipulate energy and possibility and alter physical reality from within Quantum Space.

Wizardling – A novice wizard.

Books by Dr. Mayo

This trilogy of 'Coincidental Journey,' 'Untold Story,' and 'Wizardling,' is about Lucid Dreaming, Dream-walking, Shape-shifting, Sorcery, Wizardry, Magic, Time Travel and the Powers of Illusion.

Coincidental Journey Copyright 2015
ISBN # 978-1-940985-16-9
This is the first book in the trilogy. It was completed in 2015 & is awaiting publication.

Untold Story Copyright 2016
ISBN # 978-1-940985-42-8
This is the second book in the trilogy. It was completed in 2016 & is awaiting publication.

Wizardling Copyright 2017
ISBN # 978-1-940985-73-2
This is the third book of the trilogy.
It was published and released in: April 2019

Robin Copyright 2018
ISBN # 978-1-940985-55-8
The theme of this Elizabethan book of poetry is life, death and reincarnation. 268 pages
It was published and released in: April 2018

Oracle Copyright 2018
ISBN # 978-1-940985-95-4
This book is about a real, living Oracle.
Published & released: December 2018

Vision Quest Copyright 2019
ISBN # 978-1-7345741-0-4
This book chronicles the visions of a Seer.
This book was completed in 2019. It was published
and released in: February 2020

Star Quest: Navigator Copyright 2020
ISBN # 978-1-940985-74-9
This book evaluates several earth-like exo-planets
located within their star system's life zone for possible
life forms.
Completed in 2020. Awaiting Publication.

The Art of Magic Copyright 2020
ISBN # 978-1-7345741-2-8
This book is about the 107 concessions in the 'Carnival
of Magic.'
Completed in 2020. Awaiting publication.

At the Heart of Every Story
Lies the Teller of the Tale

Dr. Mayo was born in Tucson, Arizona, where he maintains his private dental practice, which is limited to the treatment of children and special needs patients.

This book, *Vision Quest* was intended to provide me with a gateway to the twenty-six realities that make up String Theory. My 'Vision Quest' was intended to get me through those barriers created by things and then the barriers created by beliefs, then the barriers of concepts and of perceptions, all the way to the ultimate barrier, which is the Unknown. The challenge for me then became to go beyond the barrier of the unknown to reach Quantum Space, where nothing exists but infinite energy and infinite possibilities. My task then became: "To make the unknowable knowable, to make the unknown, known and to make the impossible possible.

Guiding Principles

Last night the Source insisted that I write down what he was going to tell me. This is what the Source said:

Mind your own matters.
What matters to you doesn't matter to others.
All things in their own time.
Save time for what really matters.
You cannot save others, from themselves.

Notes

Notes

Notes

Notes

Notes

Notes

CPSIA information can be obtained
at www.ICGtesting.com
Printed in the USA
FSHW020352071221
86599FS